Another Treasury of Clean Jokes

Tal D. Bonham

BROADMAN PRESS
Nashville, Tennessee

Dedicated to the Memory of

Darty F. Stowe
and
Richard and Marilyn Douglas

Friends in Christ with whom
we laughed on earth and with
whom we shall someday
celebrate at his feet

Acknowledgments

It would be impossible to acknowledge everyone who contributed to this little book of clean jokes. I heard many of them from my associates during coffee breaks. Many of them were recorded at conventions and conferences. My wife and children often share with me the latest jokes going around in their circles.

I am particularly indebted to Vicki Newberry for her help in compiling and typing the manuscript. A special word of appreciation is also due her husband, Dick, for his patience and support during this venture.

4257-06
ISBN: 0-8054-5706-2
Dewey Decimal Classification: 808.87
Subject heading: JOKES
Library of Congress Catalog Card Number: 82-73643

Printed in the United States of America

Foreword

"From the loss of a loved one to the loss of your hair—humor can help you cope with anything!"—Anonymous

Introduction

A young girl became a Christian in an exciting revival at her church and was baptized the closing Sunday morning. That afternoon she ran through the house singing and dancing.

Her sour grandfather rebuked her with these words, "You ought to be ashamed of yourself! Just joined the church and singing and dancing on the Lord's Day!"

Crushed by her grandfather's attitude, the little girl went out to the barn, climbed up on the corral fence, and observed an old mule standing there with a sad, droopy face and bleary eyes, with tears coursing down his cheeks.

As she reached over and patted the mule sympathetically, she said, "Don't cry ol' mule. I guess you have just got the same kind of religion that grandpa has!"

The teachings of the Bible are often falsely construed as joy-killing and pleasure-stifling precepts designed to make us sad and somber. But the Bible has much to say about happiness, joy, and a sense of humor.

Many doctors are now preaching the truth of Proverbs 17:22: "A merry heart doeth good like a medicine: but a broken spirit drieth the bones." They cite case after case of patients who have overcome physical ailments by learning to laugh. One doctor recently found that all of his healthy elderly patients had one thing in common—a good sense of humor.

Young medical students are being taught that helping patients to relax and laugh may do more good than some prescriptions. Psychologists are finding that those who are anxious and humorless are much more susceptible to a variety of diseases. Laughter is being dubbed "internal jogging" and "instant intellect" by many doctors. One renowned professor, recently discussing the therapeutic value of laughter at a seminar on suicide, said, "Assure your patients it's not a sin to laugh. I don't believe we know much about God if we've never heard him laugh."

If you find in this book a therapeutic tool to help you physically, emotionally, or even spiritually, it will have been worth it all!

However, I hope you will also find in this book a tremendous aid to communication. Humor encourages listening and enhances speaking. It aids in the expression of other emotions as well.

Therefore, I have compiled this little book for anyone who is interested in using clean humor to help in communicating a message. The Sunday School teacher, the minister, the schoolteacher, the student, the salesman, and the politician should find help here. The student giving his first speech in Speech I and the seasoned speaker looking for something "new" will hopefully find help in this book. As you read it, remember the words of a famous barb, "Laughter is the shortest distance between two people."

Contents

Achievement

If you want a place in the sun, you must expect to get a few blisters.

Average businessman: "I wouldn't mind the rat race so much if I could just have a little more cheese."

There was the absentminded professor who forgot to write a book to sell to his class.

Each year it takes less time to fly around the world and more time to drive to work.

The new jet age can be described as breakfast in London, luncheon in New York, dinner in San Francisco, and baggage in Buenos Aires.

Well digging is the only job left where you start at the top.

The itinerant odd-jobs man knocked on the kitchen door for his lunch.

"And did you notice that big pile of wood over there?" asked the lady.

"Yeah, I seen it."

"Mind your grammar," snapped the lady. "You should say you saw it."

"Lady," returned the man, "you saw me see it, but you ain't seen me saw it."

"Lady, if you'll give us a quarter, my little brother will imitate a chicken."

"What will he do? Cackle like a hen?"

"Oh, no. He wouldn't do a cheap imitation like that. He'll eat a worm."

Book salesman: "This do-it-yourself book will help you to run your elevator more efficiently. See, there's a whole chapter on elevators."

"I don't want no help running this elevator," replied the operator. "It runs OK now."

Persisted the salesman, "But this book will help you to run it better. You'll know twice as much when you get through reading it."

"No way," replied the operator, "I don't want to learn anything. I know more already than I get paid for."

"I really hate to tell you this, but I just ran over your cat with my car, so I'd like to replace him."

"All right. There's a mouse in the kitchen!"

A man's small son came home with twenty-five dollars which he had earned by selling magazine subscriptions.

"How many sales did it take to collect twenty-five dollars?" asked his father.

"One," he replied. "I sold all the subscriptions to one man—his dog bit me."

A young man started work as a shipping clerk in a large manufacturing plant. Within two weeks he had advanced to a salesman's position, and a month later he was promoted to sales manager. Two months later he became plant manager in charge of production. The next month he was made vice-president with a salary of $60,000 a year.

After the meeting where he had last been promoted, the president of the company shook the young man's hand and asked him to say a few words.

"Thanks!" said the new executive.

"Thanks!" exclaimed the president. "Is that all you have to say? This is one of the biggest days of your life!"

"You're right, Sir. I'm going to celebrate. Tell my Mom I'll be home late for dinner."

Success comes to him who can blow his own horn while blowing others' minds.

Give a man enough rope and he'll fill the house with potted plants in weird-looking macrame hangers.

The paths of glory lead but to the grave—so do all other paths.

Cleanliness is next to—impossible.

Advertising

Running a business without advertising is like winking at a girl in the dark—you know what you are doing but nobody else does.

Joe: "Advertising costs me a lot of money."
Ben: "Why, I've never seen your goods advertised."
Joe: "They aren't. But my wife reads other people's ads."

One of the stenographers at an insurance agency kept falling asleep at her desk. Before discharging her, the office manager and sales manager discussed the situation.

The office manager was really undecided. "But we can't let her go," he moaned. "You know we'd never be able to get another person to take her place."

Suddenly a possible solution came to the sales manager, "Why don't we print a sign to hang on her when she's sleeping at her desk? It can say: 'When you are adequately covered by insurance, you, too, will sleep this way.'"

You know, Samson had the right idea when it came to advertising. He took two columns and brought the house down.

He had been going from church to church, trying to find a friendly congregation, and finally he stopped in a little church just as the congregation read with the minister: "We have left undone those things which we ought to have done; and we have done those things that we ought not to have done."

The man slipped into a pew with a sigh of relief. *Thank goodness,* he thought, *I've found my crowd at last.*

Ad in small-town newspaper: "If Jack Smith, who deserted his wife and baby twenty years ago will return, the aforementioned baby will knock the socks off him."

When a reader called to the attention of the editor a dead spider he had found in his paper, the editor wrote, "The poor thing was just looking to see which merchants did not advertise so it could find a doorway in which to spin its web without being disturbed."

In a small store with a window on the street the owner was observed feeding a cat from a priceless antique saucer. Antique lovers would come in and buy the cat and then ask for the saucer, figuring the owner didn't know the value of the saucer.

"Of course, I couldn't sell the saucer, but I've sold twenty cats from that old saucer so far," he told a customer.

An advertising salesman arrived at a hotel and took a room. He brought with him only a small bag, and the hotel porter asked for the tags for his trunks.

"I don't have any tags," said the salesman.

"But I thought you were a salesman," said the porter.

"That's right. But I don't need any sample cases. I sell brains."

The porter thought for a moment and said, "Well, Sir, you are the first traveling salesman that's ever come here without any samples."

Reporter: "I understand you have just hired a press agent to publicize your teachings."

Philosopher: "Yes, that's right. This press agent has just been assigned to distribute my precepts to the four corners of the earth. He claims he can spread my message with great speed."

Reporter: "Could you share some of these precepts with us?"

Philosopher: "I would be delighted: 'A stitch in time saves nine'; 'A bird in the hand is worth two in the bush'; and 'A penny saved is a penny earned.'"

Reporter: "Those are very familiar sayings already."

Philosopher: "I told you he worked fast!"

"What's wrong, son?" asked Mark's father.

"I lost my puppy," cried Mark.

"Well, don't cry, we'll get your dog back. We will put an ad in the paper," replied Mark's father.

"That won't help," wailed Mark, "my dog can't read."

Advice

A well-known writer was asked, "What was the best advice you ever received?"

He answered, "To marry the girl I did."

"Who gave you that advice, Sir?"

The writer smiled wryly and replied, "She did."

Robby arrived home from school with two black eyes.

"Fighting again!" said his mother. "I thought I told you that when you were angry you should count to one hundred before you did anything."

"I know," said Robby, "but the other boy's mother told him to count to fifty."

Two bums were sitting together on a park bench. One of them said to the other, "I'm a man who never took advice from anybody."

Said the other, "Shake, old buddy, I'm the man who followed everybody's advice."

Young man in jewelry store: "Please engrave this engagement ring, 'From Tim to Cindy.'"

Jeweler: "Take some advice, son, and just have, 'From Tim.'"

Doctor: "Your husband must have peace and quiet and rest. Here are some sleeping pills."

Patient's wife: "But when should I give them to him?"

Doctor: "You don't understand—they are for you."

Patient: "How much would you charge to fix my nose?"

Doctor: "A thousand dollars."

Patient: "Anything cheaper?"

Doctor: "Well, you could try walking into a tree."

A frowning woman walked up to a little boy she had caught smoking. "Does your mother know you smoke?" she demanded.

"Lady," he countered, "does your husband know you stop and talk to strange men on the street?"

Overheard at an auction sale: "Sold—to the lady with her husband's hand over her mouth."

Motto: Keep your nose to the grindstone, your shoulder to the wheel, and your eye on the ball. Now, try to work in that position.

A young mother was quite alarmed when her young son swallowed a coin.

"Hurry, send for the doctor," she urged her husband.

"No, I think we should send for the preacher," replied the father.

"The preacher? Why, you don't think he is going to die, do you?" exclaimed the mother.

"Oh, no," the husband replied quickly. "But you know our preacher—he can get money out of anybody!"

"Can you tell me how I can cut down on my strokes while golfing?"

"Sure, take up painting."

He who says it can't be done shouldn't interrupt the one who is doing it.

Two salesmen went wild game hunting in Africa. While walking through a dense forest they came to a clearing in the jungle. Suddenly Ken whispered to Mike, who was directly in front of him, "Don't look now, but is that a lion following us?"

Whispered Sam, "Don't ask me. Do I look like a fur salesman?"

Customer: "To what do you owe your success as a door-to-door salesman?"

Salesman: "To the first words I say when a woman answers the door—"Miss, is your mother at home?"

An old salesman was giving advice to a young salesman:

"Now don't forget—never try to sell an encyclopedia to a new bride."

"But why?" asked the new salesman.

"Because a new bride thinks her husband knows everything," advised the experienced salesman.

"What luck!" exclaimed the real estate salesman who had just cleared his first deal. "The house I just sold turns out to be under water. Boss, that customer is going to be pretty upset when he finds out about it. What should I do? Give him his money back?"

"Are you crazy?" screamed the boss. "What kind of a salesman are you, anyway? Get out there and sell him a boat!"

A man who had been dating a girl for several years took her to a Japanese restaurant. After looking over the menu for several minutes he asked her, "How would you like your rice— fried or boiled?"

She looked him straight in the eye and said, "Thrown!"

When he visits a sick friend in the hospital he brings him magazines to read but advises, "If I were you, I wouldn't start any serials."

Animals

Scene: Two elephants entering Noah's ark.

One said to the other, "On the other hand, Clyde, who else has ever asked us to take a boat trip?"

A man visiting a zoo was astounded to see an orangutan with a book in each hand, reading. The man asked, "Excuse me, but are you actually reading?"

"Of course," the ape replied. "Darwin's theory of evolution and the Holy Bible."

"Well," said the man, "are you sure you understand what you are reading?"

"I'm not so sure," said the orangutan. "The more I study the more I wonder whether I'm my brother's keeper or in fact, my keeper's brother."

A mother hen was having a difficult time keeping a strong-willed chick in line, and exclaimed, "If your pa could see you now, he'd turn over in his gravy."

Keep your city clean—eat a pigeon.

Tim: "They had to shoot poor old Rover yesterday."
Dick: "Was he mad?"
Tim: "He wasn't too pleased."

One mother kangaroo to another: "I hope it doesn't rain today. I hate it when the kids play inside."

A man and his dog were playing checkers when a friend dropped by. The friend was amazed and watched for awhile. Finally he said, "That's the most intelligent dog I have ever seen."

"He's not really that smart," said the dog's owner. "I've beat him five out of six games."

A little boy was trying to make a good Baptist out of the family cat by immersing him in the bathtub. The cat started yowling, and the little boy said, "All right—be a Methodist then,"—and he let the candidate go.

A certain family had a dog named Paddy. They were very fond of the dog, especially their young son. Unfortunately, the dog was hit by a car and killed. Peter was at school, and his mother, thinking she would soften the shock a little, went to meet him and, as tactfully as she could, broke the news of Paddy's death. To her surprise, Peter took it very calmly. Later in the day, as she was busy in the house, young Peter came sobbing into the room. "Paddy's dead," he cried. "Paddy's dead." "Yes," said his mother, "but I had already told you that and you didn't pay much attention." "But I thought you said Daddy!"

A lady was having an elegant party and wanted to serve mushrooms, but was a little uncertain about them, so she gave them to the dog. He ate them and everything seemed all right, so the mushrooms were prepared and served. During the party the maid hurried to the hostess and said, "The dog is dead."

The guests hurried to the hospital and received first aid. After the confusion was over, the maid said, "That car sure did mess up the dog."

"Hello—police department? I've lost my cat and . . . "

"Sorry, but we are very busy. That's not a job for the police."

"I'm afraid you don't understand. This is a very rare cat, very intelligent. He is practically human. He can almost talk."

"Well, Sir, maybe you had better hang up. He might be trying to call you right now."

Ron: "Does your dog bite?"
Ralph: "No." (Suddenly the dog bites Ron.)
Ron: "I thought you said your dog didn't bite!"
Ralph: "That isn't my dog."

A friend of mine crossed a polar bear with a python. He doesn't know what he's got, but it makes a great rug for a long thin hallway.

What would you call a cat that likes to dig in the sand? Sandy Claws.

Pam: "Which is the cats' all-time favorite song?"
Gil: "Three Blind Mice."

Tina: "What is another name for a cat's home?"
Tammy: "A scratch pad."

Helen: "What dog is not liked by a lot of people?"
Elnora: "The Doberman, because it's a pinscher!"

Lana: "What do you feed your pet frog?"
Loretta: "Croakers and milk!"

Freda: "How do you stop a ten-pound parrot from talking too much?"
Judy: "Buy a twenty-pound cat!"

A brilliant magician was performing on an ocean liner. But every time he did a trick, a talking cat in the audience would yell, "It's a trick. He's a phony. That's not magic."

Then one evening during a storm, the ship sank while the magician was performing. And the cat and the magician ended up in the same lifeboat. For several days they just glared at each other, neither saying a word to the other. Finally the cat said, "All right, smarty, you and your stupid tricks. What did you do with the ship?"

Barbara: "Which part of the fish weighs the most?"
Caroline: "The scales."

Don: "What kind of turtle should you never trust?"
Art: "A turtle-tale."

Grady: "Doctor, you've got to help my brother! He thinks he is a dog."
Doc: "How long has this been going on?"
Grady: "Ever since he was a pup!"

Esther: "What is the difference between a cat and a comma?"
Vicki: "One means pause at the end of a clause, and the other means claws at the end of paws!"

Shirley: "Can anything be smarter than a cat that can count?"
Mabel: "Yes, a spelling bee!"

Caroline: "How can you tell if your cat can count?"
Grady: "Ask it what one minus one is, then see if the cat says nothing!"

Belinda: "If a fat cat is a flabby tabby, then what is a very small cat?"
Esther: "An itty bitty kitty."

Beverly: "What is the best award a cat can earn?"
Theo: "The Purr-litzer prize."

Anxiety

An astronaut preparing for a launch into space was asked how he felt. The astronaut replied, "How would you feel knowing you were going into space in an aircraft with over 140,000 parts and they were all supplied by the lowest bidders?"

Patient: "Doctor, you pulled the wrong tooth."
Dentist: "Don't get excited. I'll get to it."

A staunch old Republican invariably managed to show up at all the Democratic rallies. A friend suggested that perhaps he was thinking of swapping sides. The diehard snorted indignantly, "Change parties? Never! I just go to their meetings to keep my disgust fresh."

A man filling out an application in a factory was greatly perplexed at one question: "Person to notify in case of accident?"
His decision: "Anybody in sight."

The only way to get out of bed every morning with a big smile on your face is to go to bed at night with a coat hanger in your mouth.

This is the age of the pill—pills to perk you up, pills to calm you down. I asked a friend the other day how he felt. He said he didn't know because he forgot which pill he had taken.

"When I was in high school I suffered from a tremendous inferiority complex. I felt so insecure that at football games, when the team went into a huddle, I was sure they were talking about me."

Nervous man: "I've got butterflies in my stomach."
Doctor: "Here, take an aspirin."
Nervous man: "I just did. Now they're playing Ping-Pong with it.

"See that boy over there who's annoying Julie?"
"What do you mean? He isn't even looking at her."
"I know. That's what is annoying her."

Dumb blonde: "I really can't play golf. I don't even know how to hold the caddie."

Man to friend: "I think my wife is tired of me."
Friend: "What makes you think so?"
First man: "Every day this week she has wrapped my lunch in a road map."

A large department store was very crowded with shoppers. A young mother was having a difficult time with her small daughter, who kept pulling and tugging on her skirt and whining. Finally, the harrassed mother softly pleaded, "Quiet now, Cynthia, just calm down and take it easy."

A salesclerk watching commented to the little girl, "So your name is Cynthia."

"Oh, no," interrupted the mother, "her name is Amy. I'm Cynthia."

After having their fifth child, a couple received a playpen from their friends. Several weeks later the friends who sent the gift received this note of thanks: "The playpen is wonderful.

Just what we needed. I sit in it every afternoon and read—and the kids can't get close to me!"

Hypochondriac: "I feel a little better this morning, but when I feel better I always feel worse, because I know I will feel bad tomorrow."

Golfer: "That's the tenth time I've swung at that ball, and I still haven't hit it."
Friend: "Well, keep swinging. I think you've got it worried."

A man was told one morning that he looked tired. "I am tired," he said. "Last night, I was reading in a magazine that a man turns over every fifteen minutes. I weigh 200 pounds, so last night I moved 6,400 pounds and just the thought of it makes me tired."

He's as jumpy and squirmy as a long-tailed cat in a room full of rocking chairs.

More nervous than a turkey around November.

At the first sign of trouble, he thinks with his legs.

She bites her fingernails so often that her stomach needs a manicure.

He'd commit suicide if he could do it without killing himself.

She's so nervous she can thread the needle of a sewing machine while it is turned on.

Bravery

A frightened man said to the flight attendant upon leaving a plane that had flown through a thunderstorm, "Thanks for the rides."

"What are you talking about?" she asked. "You only had one ride."

"That's what you think! I have just had my first and my last plane ride," he replied.

A United States pilot in Hong Kong met a fellow who claimed he had been a kamikaze pilot in World War II. "War all over now," he said. "We be friends—my name Chow Mein."

"But kamikaze flyers were suicide pilots," said the American. "If you really had been one, you'd be dead now."

The former kamikaze smiled wryly, "Me chicken Chow Mein."

"Why," asked the policeman, "did you kick this man in the stomach?"

"Because," said the culprit, "he turned around."

The application for a new driver's license asked the following question: "Have you ever been arrested?"

The applicant answered: "No."

The next question was: "State why."

The applicant answered: "Never been caught."

At a church picnic Mrs. Benson won the rolling pin throwing contest, and Mr. Benson won the fifty yard dash.

"All right, Charlie," said the robber to his partner. "I want you to walk inside the bank, and if anyone gets in your way, shoot him down. Grab all the money, come walking outside. I'll be sitting in the getaway car. And remember one thing— I'll be taking all the chances."

"You mean to tell me," asked his pal, "that you want me to walk inside the bank, and if anyone gets in my way, shoot him down, grab all the money, and come walking outside? You'll be waiting in the car for me, and you say you'll be taking all the chances? What chances are you talking about?"

"The biggest one of all," answered the leader. "I can't drive!"

A bridegroom was embarrassed by being called upon for a speech at the wedding rehearsal dinner. He put his trembling hand on the shoulder of his bride-to-be and stammered, "This thing has been forced upon me. I really did not expect it."

Sunday School teacher to class of young boys—"Who went into the lion's den and came out unhurt?"
Answer—"Tarzan!"

A missionary unexpectedly met a lion in the jungle. Not seeing any way to escape, he fell to his knees in prayer. He was comforted by seeing the lion kneeling next to him.

"Dear Brother, how delightful to join you in prayer when only a moment ago I feared for my life," the missionary said.

"Don't interrupt," said the lion, "I'm just saying grace."

The world will usually forgive you for being blue, sometimes for being green, but never for being yellow.

"Could I see the captain of this ship, please?"
"Miss, he's forward."
"That's OK. I'm not afraid. I've never met a man I couldn't handle."

"I've just come from the upper peninsula with 100 deer!" declared a brave hunter.

"Do you know who I am?"

"No."

"Well, I'm the game warden of this state, and you are under arrest for violating the law."

"Do you know who I am?"

"I haven't the faintest idea."

"Why, I'm the biggest liar in Ohio!"

The boat was sinking. The captain called out, "Does anyone here know how to pray?"

"I do," replied a voice in the rear.

"OK, you pray. The rest of us will put on life jackets. We're short one."

Bulletins

We'll pass through the most gigantic dust storm in history when all church members dust off their Bibles at the same time.

He was in the habit of opening his Bible at random and taking the first thing his eyes fell on as something that would be helpful to him.

One day the verse he read was, "Judas . . . went and hanged himself."

Not thinking that quite suitable, he shut the Bible and opened it again at another place. The verse his eyes fell on was, "Go and do thou likewise."

He tried again. This time he read, "That thou doest, do quickly."

The Sunday before Easter the junior choir sang at the regular service. After their last number, and while the pastor was stepping up to the pulpit, one small singer got up and walked out.

"I guess," the minister observed, "he's used to leaving the room during the commercials."

A church service is always much more meaningful and interesting when the sermon and music go together. Too many times they appear to be separate services, with no apparent connection. One preacher was very enthusiastic about having the music supplement the Scripture text, and usually he and the music director had the program definitely harmonized and planned in advance.

However, on one occasion they neglected to do this. In this situation, the preacher chose for his subject the beautiful story of an ailing woman of great faith, who was healed merely by touching the garment of the Master as he passed by. The preacher closed with the words of Jesus, "Who touched me?" From the choir loft came the refrain, "Search Me, O, Lord."

New choir member: "What is your position in the choir?"
Gentle-mannered bass: "Neutral. I don't side with either faction."

There was quite a bit of confusion in a church after the morning bulletin read: "Text for today, 'Thou Shalt Not Steal.' The choir will sing, 'Steal, Steal Away.'"

This new collection box has some unique features. When you drop a quarter or more it doesn't make a sound. Drop a dime and it tinkles like a bell. A nickel blows a whistle, and a penny fires a shot. And when you don't put anything in—the box takes your picture.

On Sunday morning at a Texas prison, a group of inmates were being led to the Catholic and Protestant chapels. One prisoner did not enter either chapel but kept on walking toward the main gate. A guard caught up with him and asked, "Where are you going?"

The prisoner replied, "I was told I could go to the church of my choice—and that is in San Antonio!"

Cheerfulness

Three elderly men were passing the time discussing the ideal way of leaving this world. The first, age seventy-five, remarked he'd like to go quickly and suggested a crash in a speeding car. The second, age eighty-five, agreed on a speedy end but thought he'd prefer a plane crash.

"I've got a better idea," mused the third, age ninety-five. "I'd rather be shot by a jealous husband."

"What do you think of Medicare?" someone asked a sweet, elderly lady.

"Oh, it's just wonderful," she answered. "I've had one bottle, and I'm feeling better already."

A young lady boarded the bus after the lights had gone out. A tall man standing near her asked if he could help her find a strap.

"Thank you," she replied, "but I have already found one."

"Then I wonder if you would mind letting go of my necktie!"

The clerk in a book store told a college student, "Here is a book that will do half your work for you."

The student replied, "That's great. I'll take two of them."

A mental patient walked up to the new administrator of the state hospital. "We like you much better than we did the last guy," he said.

The new administrator smiled and said, "Why is that?"

"Oh, you seem more like one of us."

A minister was visiting some of his members one afternoon. As he knocked on one woman's door, she called out, "Angel, is that you?"

The minister replied, "No—but I'm from the same department!"

"I wish you would show a little more sensitivity," said the restaurant manager to the leader of the orchestra. "We had the Society of Umbrella and Raincoat Manufacturers having dinner here this evening, and you had the band play 'It Ain't Gonna Rain No More.'"

A salesman had tried with no success for five years to sell a certain prospect. After each turndown the salesman would tell the prospect, "I wish I had seventy-five like you."

At last the customer became curious and asked him why he always said the same thing after each call. The salesman replied, "Because I have 150 like you, but I wish I only had seventy-five."

Somebody needs to tell us it only takes fifteen facial muscles to smile and sixty-five facial muscles to frown. Then maybe we would stop overworking ourselves.

Children

A little boy who lived a sheltered life in the country came to town one Saturday with his mother and saw, for the first time, several bowlegged cowboys standing out in front of the general store. "Look at all those bowlegged cowboys!" the little boy exclaimed.

When he got home, his father punished him for the brash remarks concerning the cowboys by making him read Shakespeare one hour every day for the next several months.

When they returned to the little town months later, the same bowlegged cowboys were standing out in front of the general store. The little boy, without thinking, screamed, "Look at all those. . . . " He corrected himself in the middle of the sentence and said, "Hark, what manner of men are these, who wear their knees in parentheses?"

His parents always signed his grade card with an X so the teacher wouldn't know that anyone who could read and write had a son like that.

A teacher had just given her class a lesson on magnets. In the follow-up test, one question read, "My name starts with 'M,' has six letters, and I pick up things. What am I?"

She was a bit surprised to find half the class answered the question with the word "Mother."

A mother was worried about her eight-year-old son. No matter how often she scolded him, he kept running around with his shirttail hanging out of his pants.

Her neighbor had three boys, and each kept his shirt tucked in neatly. Finally the woman asked her neighbor to tell her the secret.

"It is very simple," she answered. "I just sew a bit of lace around the bottoms of their shirts."

A small boy, visiting New York City for the first time, went in an elevator to the top of a very tall building. As he shot past the sixty-second floor at a breathtaking speed, he gulped, turned to his father and asked, "Daddy, does God know we are coming?"

"There were only three boys in school today who could answer one question that the teacher asked," said a small, proud boy to his mother.

"I hope you were one of them," said his mother.

"Oh, I was, and Bobby Miller and Johnny Smith were the other two."

"Well, I'm very proud of you. What question did your teacher ask?"

"Who broke the window at recess?"

Inquired the teacher of a Sunday School class, "Have any of you ever seen an elephant's skin?"

"I have," exclaimed one small girl.

"Where?" asked the teacher.

"On the elephant."

Jimmy brought home his report card, and his father wasn't very pleased. "Just look at Tommy Sparks," remarked the father, "he is always at the head of his class."

"But, Dad, you have to remember, he has really smart parents."

A minister's young daughter had to go to bed early because she was not feeling well; therefore, she missed her usual playtime with her daddy. A few minutes later, she came to the top of the stairs and called, "Mommy, I need to talk to Daddy."

"No, honey," her mother replied, "get back in bed."

"Mommy, please."

"No, I said, now that's enough."

"Mother, I am a very ill woman, and I need to speak with my pastor right away."

Sometimes bending a child over has a strange way of straightening him out.

It was an exceptionally hot day, and they were having company for dinner. Mother asked five-year-old Jason to say the prayer before they ate.

"But what should I say?" asked Jason.

"Just say what you hear me say," said his mother.

Little Jason bowed his head and said, "Dear Lord, why did I ever invite people over on a hot day like this?"

Little girl: "I'm in love with a boy in my class, and I'm going to marry him."

Mother: "That's wonderful. Does he have a job?"

Little girl: "Oh, yes! He erases the blackboard for our class."

Mikey and his mother were in the grocery store, and a clerk handed Mikey a candy bar.

"What do you say?" asked Mikey's mother.

Mikey replied, "Charge it!"

Mother: "Why did you fall in the mud puddle with your dress on?"

Annie: "There wasn't time to take it off."

Six-year-old Jenny complained to her mother of a stomachache. Her mother replied, "That's because your stomach is empty. You'd feel better if there were something in it."

That evening their pastor stopped for a visit and said his head had hurt him all day. Little Jenny quickly advised, "That's because it's empty. You'd feel better if there was something in it."

"How old are you, Jeremy?" asked Mr. Anderson.

"Well," said little Jeremy, "when I'm home I'm thirteen, when I'm at school I'm fourteen, and when I go to the movies I'm twelve."

After a warning that a tornado was approaching, a young couple sent their small son to an uncle who lived out of the danger zone. A few hours later they received a telegram stating: "Am returning your boy. Please send tornado instead."

Sunday School teacher: "Why did Mary and Joseph take Jesus with them to Jerusalem?"
Little Joanie: "Maybe they couldn't get a baby-sitter?"

A family moved into a new, modern home in a new housing area. Many modern appliances were delivered to the home. One neighbor asked another, "Is everything in that home run by the switch?"

The other neighbor, who had been watching their children playing in the yard, spoke up and said, "Everything but the children."

A little boy was spelling banana. He started off, "ba-na-na-na-na."

"Don't you know how to spell banana?" asked his teacher.

"Sure I do. But I don't know when to stop."

A father was surprised at the difference in the dispositions of his two sons. One was a confirmed optimist and the other a pessimist. He decided to put them to a test and see how far they would carry these traits. On Christmas morning the two boys came downstairs to see what Santa had brought them. The father hid behind the door and watched them. In one boy's stocking was only a piece of leather halter and a small horsewhip. The other boy's stocking was overflowing with gifts. This latter boy, who was the pessimist, looked over his array of presents with a bit of sadness. "What did you get?" asked his cheerful brother. "Not much, just the usual—games and things—nothing I really care about. How about you?" Replied the optimist, "I got a pony, but it ran away."

UPI reported the following medical techniques derived from a first aid test by a fourth grade class in Edmonds, Washington:

For head colds: "Use an agonizer to spray the nose until it drops in the throat."

For nosebleed: "Put the nose lower than the body."

For fractures: "To see if the limb is broken, wiggle it gently back and forth."

For asphyxiation: "Apply artificial respiration until the victim's dead."

Moral: Don't ever require first aid while on an elementary playground.

Clarity

A young man asked the older fellow next to him on the bus for the time.

"Tell you the time?" the fellow exclaimed. "I should say not! Why, if I were to tell you the time, I'd probably ask you to have a cup of coffee with me, since you seem like such a nice young man. If we drank coffee I would probably follow up with a dinner invitation. When we got home, you would probably be interested in my young daughter. You would probably want to marry her, and she would most likely accept. And if you think I want a son-in-law who can't even afford a watch of his own, you've got another think coming! So why should I tell you the time?"

Clerk in book store: "What is the name of your church, Sir?"
Customer: "Black Walnut Baptist Church, you know, as in ice cream."

Pat: "Do you know the difference between pneumonia and ammonia?"
Jill: "Of course, one comes in chests and the other in bottles."

"Mark, if you had more spunk you would stand better in your classes. Do you know what spunk is?"
Mark (recalling past experiences): "Oh, yes, Dad. It's the past participle of spank."

A small church was having a business meeting. One member stood up and suggested that the church buy a chandelier. Another stood and said he was against it. "Why?" asked the pastor.

"Nobody can spell it; nobody can play it; and what we need most of all is more light," explained the confused member.

College senior to freshman date: "Do you enjoy Kipling?"
Young freshman: "I don't know—how do you kipple?"

Policeman: "When I saw you coming around the corner, I said to myself, 'forty-five at least.'"
Woman driver: "Well, you are a long way off! It's this hat that makes me look so old!"

Timmy and his mother were looking through old pictures. They came upon one of a handsome young man.
"Who is that?" asked Timmy.

"That's your father," replied the mother proudly.

"Oh yeah?" said Timmy doubtfully. "Well, then who's that bald-headed man that lives with us?"

Secretary to boss: "There is a man outside who wants to see you about a bill you owe him. He wouldn't give his name."

Boss: "Well, what does he look like?"

Secretary: "He looks as if you had better pay him."

A newspaper copyreader couldn't believe it when he read a reporter's story about the theft of 2,025 pigs. "That's a lot of pigs," he growled and called the farmer to check the copy.

"Is it true that you lost 2,025 pigs?" he asked.

"Yeth," lisped the farmer.

"Thanks," said the wise copyreader and corrected the copy to read, "two sows and 25 pigs."

A fellow was accosted on the street by a holdup man. The robber said, "Stick 'em down."

"You mean 'stick 'em up'?" answered the victim.

"Oh, so that's it," replied the crook. "No wonder I haven't been making any money."

One of the fads of our day is to "return to nature." One young couple decided that they would move out of the inner city into a little country home. They could not afford to buy, so they finally found one they could rent.

As they moved into their new home in the country, they discovered there was no commode in the bathroom. The young wife thought it would be wise if they would write a letter to the landlord in a neighboring city to explain the situation. She felt quite embarrassed about complaining that there was no bathroom commode so she decided to abbreviate the two words with "B. C."

Upon receiving the letter, the landlord pondered the initials "B. C." quite some time and finally decided that the young renters were talking about a Baptist church.

So taking her "B. C." to mean "Baptist church," the landlord sat down and penned the following letter:

Dear Friend,

I regret very much the delay in answering your letter, but I take great pleasure in telling you the B. C. is located nine miles from your home and is capable of seating 250 people.

This is very unfortunate indeed if you are in the habit of going regularly, but, no doubt, you will be interested to know a great number of people take a lunch and make a day of it.

They usually arrive early and stay late. The last time my wife and I went was six years ago, and we had to stand up the whole time.

It may interest you to know a fund drive has been planned to raise money to buy new seats.

I would like to say it pains me very much not to be able to go more regularly, but it is surely not lack of desire on my part. As we grow older it seems more of an effort—particularly in cold weather.

May I hope to see you there!

Sincerely yours,

Your landlord

A woman was getting ready for work one morning after breakfast when she heard the garbage truck coming down the street. Frantically, she ran to the door with her hair still in curlers and without any makeup.

"Am I too late for the garbage?" she asked the garbage man.

"No, lady, jump in!"

Teacher: "When does a book become a classic?"
Student: "When people who haven't read it begin to say they have."

Missionary: "Why are you looking at me so intently?"
Cannibal: "I'm the food inspector."

One parent to another: "Do you believe in spanking children?"
Other parent: "Certainly not. But I do believe in patting them on the back every once in awhile—often enough, low enough, and hard enough."

A lady standing in her kitchen was showing her friend a neighbor's wash hanging on a clothesline. "As you can see, Mrs. Simmons isn't very clean. Just look at all those streaks on her wash!"

Her friend replied, "Those streaks aren't on your neighbor's wash—they are on your window!"

A young girl went to the library searching for a book to take with her on her vacation.

"Here's a good one," said the librarian, *"The Kentucky Cardinal."*

"No, thank you. I'm not interested in religious subjects," replied the young girl.

"But this 'Kentucky Cardinal' is a bird," explained the librarian.

"I don't care about his private life either!" said the girl.

In a civil service examination for those wanting to join the Los Angeles Police Force, the following are some of the actual answers given to the questions asked:

Question: What would you do in case of a race riot?
Answer: Get the number of both cars.

Question: What is sabotage?

Answer: Breaking the laws of the sabbath.

Question: What are rabies, and what would you do for them?

Answer: Rabies are Jewish priests, and I would not do anything for them.

"My wife doesn't understand me," he complained. Turning to his closest friend, again he cried, "My wife doesn't understand me! Does yours?"

"I don't know," his friend replied, "she never mentions you."

Many years ago in Duluth, Minnesota, a Jew was run over in the iron mines. They took him to a Catholic hospital, where an Episcopal doctor cut off his leg. There a Presbyterian woman, feeling sorry for the man, wrote to the editor of a Congregational paper in Chicago, asking him to put an advertisement in his paper asking someone to donate a wooden leg to this Jew in the Catholic hospital, whose leg had been cut off by the Episcopal doctor. A Methodist woman in River Forest, Illinois, saw the advertisement in the Congregational paper. Her late husband, who had been a Baptist, had had a wooden leg. She telephoned for the Salvation Army captain to come by and wrap up her Baptist husband's wooden leg. He took it down to the express office, where a Lutheran express messenger delivered it to an Evangelical nurse in the Duluth office. She took it to the Catholic hospital, and when they strapped it on the Jew, they said he had become a United Brethren.

The judge faced the jury and angrily asked, "In view of the evidence, what possible excuse can you give for acquitting this man?"

"Insanity, Your Honor," replied the foreman.

"All of you? All twelve of you?" cried the judge.

Dan: "Dad, when did you learn to do frog impressions?"
Dad: "I don't know what you are talking about."
Dan: "Well, Mom said when you croak we'll all be rich."

Complaints

Customer: "The hot dogs you sold me the other day were meat on one end and cornmeal on the other."
Butcher: "Yes, I know. In times like these it's hard to make both ends meat."

Taxpayer: "I'm so broke after paying my income tax that I'm being supported by an orphan in Vietnam."

After receiving the bill from his dentist for having a tooth pulled, the man called the dentist and said, "This bill is three times as much as you usually charge."

"I know," said the dentist, "but you screamed so loud you scared two other patients away."

Shawn: "Do you know what it means when the preacher takes off his watch and lays it on the podium?"
Jackie: "Yep—nothing."

Daddy asked Julie if she liked her first church service. "I liked the music," she replied, "but the commercial was too long."

Preacher: "The people in this church are so thoughtful. They are dedicating a plaque to those who have died in the service."
Church member: "Which service—morning or evening?"

A woman was complaining about the bad manners of a friend who had recently visited. She said to her husband, "That woman is so rude—she must've yawned a dozen times while I was talking."

"Honey," replied her husband, "maybe she wasn't yawning. Maybe she was just trying to get a word in."

Teacher: "Jeff, your handwriting is awful. You must learn to write better."

Jeff: "I'll try, but then you'll complain about the way I spell!"

"Waiter!" shouted an angry customer. "I can't tell if this is coffee or tea. It tastes like motor oil."

"Well, if it tastes like motor oil then it's coffee, because our tea tastes like turpentine."

Mother: "Stevie, last night there were two pieces of pie in the pantry, and now there is only one. Can you explain that?"

Stevie: "Well, I guess I just didn't see the other piece."

A city farmer took a young man out to his farm one day to let him observe feeding the stock. The farmer became ill and asked the young man to feed his animals while he waited in the pickup truck.

"Did you feed my geese?" he asked the young man upon his return.

"Yes," the young man replied.

"What did you feed them?" asked the farmer.

"A bale of hay," was his reply.

"A bale of hay!" exclaimed the exasperated farmer. "Did they eat it?"

"I don't know if they ate it or not but they sure were talking about it!"

Computers have advanced far beyond man's imagination. In fact, they have advanced so far they have become a lot like men. They not only talk to each other now, but latest reports reveal that they have started blaming their mistakes on each other.

Things are so expensive today that it's cheaper to eat money. I went into a supermarket the other day and asked for two dollars worth of potatoes. The clerk said, "Sorry, but we don't slice them."

I asked for two dollars worth of Swiss cheese; he wrapped up six holes.

Milk has gone up, too. Now I don't mind cows being contented, but do they have to be hilarious?

Nowadays, apples are so expensive you might as well have the doctor a day.

Minister to garage mechanic: "Your estimate runneth over."

Three monks, members of an order which had a rule of silence, asked the abbot's permission to speak with one another. The abbot granted the oldest monk the privilege to speak one sentence that year on a coming feast day. He granted the youngest the right to speak one sentence on that feast day one year later. The third brother was to wait still another year for his feast day privilege.

Following breakfast the first year the oldest monk said, "I hate oatmeal."

A year went by, and after breakfast the youngest brother said, "I like oatmeal."

Another year passed and the third monk said, "I'm getting awfully tired of this constant bickering over oatmeal."

A citizen was serenaded by a little street band. Beckoning to the leader, he said, "I want to engage you right now to play at my funeral."

"Pleased, I assure you," murmured the leader, "but why are we so highly honored?"

"I want everyone to be genuinely sorry I'm dead," said the serenaded citizen.

An airline ticket agent was having a hard time with a man who complained about the departure times. He said, "Young woman, I could stick some feathers in my ears and get there sooner."

The agent calmly replied, "Well, Sir, the runways are clear!"

Housewife (answering the telephone): "Congratulations! You are the fiftieth pest who has tried selling me something over the phone this week."

"I just bought a two-story house. The salesman told me one story before I bought it and another story after I bought it."

The young salesman was depressed and was seeking advice from an older salesman who had more than twenty-five years experience.

"What's the problem?" asked the older salesman.

"Why is it that everytime I make a call I get insulted?" asked the young man.

"I don't understand that kind of treatment. I've been thrown out the door, hit on the head, called dirty names, but I've never been insulted!"

A salesman joined the police force. Several months later a friend asked, "How do you like being a policeman?"

Answered the new policeman, "The pay is good and the hours aren't bad, but best of all—the customer is always wrong."

When he finishes eating, the waitresses always asks him, "Was *anything* all right?"

One time he was sick at home for a week, and his secretary sent a sympathy card to his wife.

He's very quick on the flaw.

Compliments

Woman to pastor: "You don't know how much your sermons have meant to my husband since he lost his mind."

A panhandler walked up to a man and begged for money for a cup of coffee, which was promptly given. Next day the man ran into the panhandler again and inquired, "Did you enjoy the coffee?"

"Drop dead!" the bum yelled, looking the man straight in the eye. "It kept me awake all night!"

A cowboy who had done pretty well ran across an old friend who had come on hard times and had become a hobo. The cowboy handed a ten dollar bill to his former pal.

"Only ten dollars," whined the ungrateful bum. "Last time you gave me fifty dollars."

"Well, since then I got married, and we just had twins, so the expenses are mounting up," the cowboy explained.

"Oh," grumbled the hobo, "raising a family on my dough, huh?"

A minister who had kept a rather tight schedule began to feel guilty about giving his secretary so much work to do. In a lighthearted moment one day he wrote her the following memo, hoping it would cheer her up:

> They say that you shall never see
> A poem as beautiful as a tree
> But you're going to take this poem
> And like it—see
> Cause I'm so busy
> I can't give you a tree.

The next day the following verse was lying on his desk:

> I'm sure as sure can be
> That from my preacher
> I'd never ask a tree
> And poems are written
> By fools like me
> Sounds like you'd better
> Stick to your preaching, see!

A famous clergyman told his congregation, "Every blade of grass is a sermon."

A few days later a parishioner saw him mowing his lawn. "That's right, Reverend," the man said, "cut your sermons short."

Visitor to art museum: "Why did they hang this picture?"
Friend: "They must not have been able to find the artist!"

"Josh, how do you like your new baby sister?"
"Well, she's all right. But just like my dad says, there are lots of things we needed worse."

Customer in restaurant: "Didn't you hear me say well done?"
Waiter (ignoring rare steak): "Yes, Sir. Thank you so much. It's not often that we get any thanks."

"Did you tell the photographer you didn't want your picture taken?"

"Yes, I did."

"Was he offended?"

"No, he said he couldn't blame me."

"I've been taking lessons in golf. I've already spent $2,500."

"Boy, that's terrible. You should call my brother."

"Why, is he a golf pro?"

"No, he's a lawyer, and he could help you get your money back."

A saleslady in a hat shop gushed, "That's a sweet hat. Honestly, it makes you look ten years younger!"

The customer retorted, "Well, I don't want it then. I can't afford to put on ten years every time I take my hat off."

Country

Teacher (pointing to flag): "Amy, do you know what this is?"

Amy: "Yes, it is the flag of our country."

Teacher: "Now, tell me the name of our country."

Amy: "Tis of thee."

An elderly farmer wrote to a mail-order house as follows: "Please send me one of the coal stoves you show on page 317 of your catalog, and if it's any good, then I'll send you a check."

Soon he received this reply from the company, "Please send the check first. If it is any good, then we'll send the stove."

Professor: "What could be more sad than 'a man without a country'?"

Girl: "A country without a man."

A traveling salesman was stranded in a small village. He asked one of the locals if there was a movie in town. "No, Sir," came the answer.

"Any pool rooms?"

"No, Sir."

"Any bowling alleys?"

"No, Sir."

"There must be some type of amusement in this community," the salesman declared. "Surely you can suggest something."

The villager thought for a moment. "Why don't you come down to the drugstore?" he suggested. "There is a freshman home from college."

The traveler in one of the more arid plains of the Southwest asked a native, "Doesn't it ever rain here?"

After reflecting a moment, the native replied, "I wouldn't say it never rains here. Remember the story about Noah's ark when it rained for forty days and nights?"

"Sure do," replied the traveler.

"Well," said the native, "we got a quarter of an inch that time."

A man had been urged to attend the funeral of his neighbor's fourth wife. "I'm just not going," he told his own wife.

"But why not," she asked.

"Well, Martha, I'm beginning to feel a little funny 'bout going so often without anything of the same sort to ask him back to."

Back in the mountains they were having an old-fashioned revival. A big, tall, barefooted mountaineer with unusually big feet came into the church and during the revival service was moved to come up to the altar. He knelt at the kneeling bench, and an old deacon, who was blind, came over to him, placed his arm around his shoulder, and began to pray. "God bless this man who has come to confess his sins," he prayed. Then, as his arm dropped, his hand fell upon the big feet of the mountaineer. Resting his palm on the mountaineer's heels, he continued to pray, "And Lord, bless his two little boys that he has brought with him."

The traveling inspector was visiting the little country school, and the children were rather nervous. "Who wrote *Hamlet*?" he asked the most timid boy in the class.

"It wasn't me, Sir," replied the young boy.

That evening the inspector was having dinner in the home of the mayor of the village and, to make conversation, said, "This morning in school I asked one of the little boys who wrote *Hamlet* and he said, 'It wasn't me, Sir.'"

The mayor looked thoughtful for a moment and said cheerfully, "Ah, that's good. And I bet the little one had done it all the time."

The man was having trouble driving. It was dark, and the rain was coming down in sheets. There was a high wind blowing, and visibility was almost zero.

"This is a bad one," he told his pet dog, Rover, who went along with him on all his trips. "Looks like we're in for a long night."

No sooner had he said this when he spotted a small motel by the side of the road in the middle of nowhere. What luck! He drove up and parked in front of the office, took his dog in his arms, and walked in.

"I'd like a room for the night," he told the proprietor.

"Sorry, Sir," said the man at the desk, "we're all filled up."

"I could sleep on the couch," suggested the desperate traveler.

"But that's where I sleep."

"But, how can you turn me away on a night like this?" he protested.

The man at the desk just shrugged, and the traveler turned

to leave; but the proprietor stopped him before he got to the door.

"Just a minute, mister," he said. "Leave the pup here. I wouldn't turn a dog out on a night like this."

Traveling salesman: "I'll give you $100 trade-in allowance for your old carpet sweeper."

Man: "That really is tempting, but I just can't. I took her for better or worse."

Insurance salesman: "How would your wife carry on if you should die?"

Man: "Well, I don't guess that's any concern of mine as long as she behaves herself while I'm alive."

A man was charged with shooting some pigeons that belonged to a farmer. A lawyer tried to frighten the farmer.

"Now," said the counselor, "are you prepared to swear that this man shot your pigeons?"

"I didn't say he shot 'em," replied the farmer. "I said I suspected him of doing it."

"Ah! Now we are coming to it. What made you suspect him?"

"First off, I caught him on my land with a gun. Second, I heard a gun go off and saw some pigeons fall. And third, I found four of my pigeons in his pocket, and I don't think the birds flew there and committed suicide."

In a courtroom in a small town, a lawyer was questioning a witness.

"I understand you called the plaintiff."

"Yes," answered the man.

"What did you say?"

The prosecutor leaped to his feet and bellowed, "That

question is false, misleading, and tends to incriminate an entirely innocent party. The attorney for the defense is using illegal tactics. Besides being an immoral person, he is guilty of malicious practices in trying to introduce such testimony."

The lawyer jumped on the prosecutor, and the two men slugged it out all over the courtroom. The judge rapped for order, and finally court attendants separated the two members of the bar. Each man had a bloody nose and two black eyes. Then the judge ruled that if the lawyer would repeat the question the witness was required to answer it.

"I repeat, then," said the lawyer, wiping blood from his lip, "what did you say?"

"I didn't say anything," answered the witness, "he wasn't at home."

Courage

Young girl to date: "Aren't you getting embarrassed? That's the fifth time you've gone for more food."

Young man: "Why should I be embarrassed? I just tell them I'm getting it for you!"

A beggar asked for fifty cents for a cup of coffee. A well-dressed businessman gave him the fifty cents, then stopped short and said, "But I thought coffee was only a quarter."

"It is," said the beggar, "but I've got a date."

I told Danny that for every tooth he lost, a good fairy would leave a quarter under his pillow. That same afternoon he went into business—pulled out all his teeth. Today he's the only kid in the neighborhood using Polident.

A minister reprimanded a young girl for playing bits of snappy music on Sunday. "Young woman," he said, "don't you know the Ten Commandments?"

Answered the young girl, "I'm not sure. If you'll hum a few bars, I'll try to pick it up as we go."

I've never had a car accident myself, except one—a head-on crash. It wasn't my fault. It was that sign on the highway. It said, "Do not cross the line if yellow." I showed 'em I wasn't.

I was so timid that I wouldn't take a bath unless my mother blindfolded the rubber duck, and I'd never undress in front of the princess telephone.

A man called all of his creditors together to tell them he was going bankrupt.

"I owe you over two hundred thousand dollars, and my assets aren't enough to pay ten cents on the dollar. So I guess it will be impossible for you to get anything—unless you want to cut me up and divide me among you."

One of the creditors spoke up, "I make a motion we do it. I'd like to have his gall."

A boy was asked how he had become such an excellent skater. He replied, "By getting up every time I fell down."

Curiosity

A religious book store had a display of communion ware on the table. A little boy was looking at one of the bases on which the trays were stacked. Curiosity got the best of him, and finally he asked the salesclerk, "Is that a hub cap?"

A father took his daughter to see her first ballet. After watching the girls dancing on their toes all evening, the little girl asked, "Why don't they just get taller dancers?"

Son: "Daddy, what are ancestors?"
Father: "Well, I am your ancestor, and so is your grandfather."
Son: "Well, then why do people always brag about them?"

Two men were traveling together on a plane. One, hoping to break the ice, asked his fellow traveler for a match to light his pipe. After the man's pipe was lit they began talking.
"What kind of business are you in?" asked the first.
"This might sound strange, but I'm a pepper seller."
The first man held out his hand, "Shake. I'm a salt seller."

A man went up to the desk to register for a room in a motel. As he picked up the pen a bedbug crawled across the desk.
"I've stayed in a lot of motels, and I've been bitten by a lot of bedbugs. But this is the first time one ever came down to see what room I was getting."

Todd bought a green shirt with big purple polka dots on it. Inside the pocket he found a note with a girl's name and address and a request that the buyer of the shirt send a picture of himself.

Ah, romance, thought Todd, as he addressed the envelope and mailed the picture.

Several days later he received a reply. He anxiously opened the envelope and found a note that read:

"Thanks for the picture. I was just curious to see what kind of a jerk would buy that kind of shirt."

A kindhearted old gentleman saw a little boy trying to reach a doorbell. The elderly man rang the bell and asked, "What now, little boy?"

"Run," said the boy, "that's what I'm gonna do."

An Eskimo mother was sitting in the igloo and reading from a storybook to her small son. "Little Jack Horner," she read, "sat in a corner."

"Mother," asked the small boy, "what's a corner?"

A father was scolding his young son for telling lies. "I never told lies when I was your age," he said.

Replied the young son, "How old were you when you started?"

A man who hadn't lived the best kind of life had passed away. At his funeral the pastor gave a nice description of the man, telling what a good husband and father he had been. After listening for awhile, the wife leaned over to her daughter and whispered, "Go over there and see if that's your father in that coffin."

The little girl asked her mother at dinner, "Isn't this roast pork we are having?"

"Yes it is. Why do you ask?"

She looked at the minister who was having dinner with them and replied, "Daddy is so silly. He said we were going to have old muttonhead for dinner this evening!"

A mother was starting out of the house to attend a party. One of her seven children said, "Mother, please let us go with you."

"No, children, this is a surprise party," she told them.

The child thought for a moment and said, "Wouldn't the lady be more surprised if you brought the seven of us along?"

"Twins?" asked the visiting minister.

"Yes," replied the mother, "both boys."

"How do you tell them apart?" asked the pastor.

"This one," said the mother, pointing, "is this, and that one is that one there."

"But," said the minister, pointing, "couldn't this one be this, also?"

"Yes," said the mother, "then, of course, that one could be that."

"How do you manage to separate them?"

"We seldom do," explained the mother, "but when we want to, we put one in one room and the other twin in another room."

"How do you know which one you're putting in each room?"

"We look and see which is in the other room and then we know the other is in the other room."

"But if one of them was in the house, and the other was away somewhere, would you be able to tell which was in the house?"

"Oh, yes," said the mother. "We'd just look at him and then we'd know the one we saw was the one in the house. Naturally, the one away somewhere would be the other. There are only two of them, which makes it easy."

"Yes," wailed the pastor, "if they were quintuplets it would have driven me out of my mind!"

Definitions

AMISS—A woman who is not married.

ATP—What Indians live in.

ADULT—One who stopped growing except in the middle.

ANT—A small insect, always working, but still finds times to go on picnics.

BABY-SITTER—Someone you pay to watch your television and eat your food.

BACHELOR—Footloose and fiancée free.

BUDGET—A family quarrel.

BUS DRIVER—One who only thought he liked children.

BUDGETING—Orderly way to get into debt.

BREAKING POINT—Moment when you stop trying to balance the budget and start trying to budget the balance.

BRAT—A child who acts like your own but belongs to someone else.

BABY—An angel whose wings grow shorter as their legs grow longer.

BOSS—The one who is early when you are late and late when you are early.

BOY—A noise with dirt on it.

BUDGET—A lot of figures that prove you should never have gotten married in the first place.

CAR SICKNESS—How you feel each month when the payment is due.

CAVITY—An empty space waiting to be filled with dentist bills.

CHEF—A man with a vocabulary big enough to give a different name to soup every day.

CHILD—The thing that stands between an adult and the television set.

CHILDISH GAMES—Those at which your wife beats you.

CIRCUS—A group that carries on where Congress leaves off.

CITY LIFE—Thousands of people being lonesome together.

COACH—A man who will gladly lay down your life for the team.

DANDRUFF—Chips off the old block.

DOCTOR—The man who tells you if you don't cut out something, he'll be cutting something out of you.

DRUGSTORE—Poor man's country club.

DESK—A trash can with drawers.

DEATH—When you stop sinning suddenly.

DIET—What you keep putting off while you keep putting on.

DIETING—The victory of mind over platter.

DIPLOMAT—A man who can convince his wife that women look fat in furs.

EASY CHAIR—The one that is never empty.

EDUCATION—What is left over after you have the facts.

EULOGY—Adoration that is long overdue.

EXPERIENCE—What makes somebody make new mistakes instead of repeating old ones.

FARM—What a city man dreams about at 5:00 PM but never at 5:00 AM.

FLASHLIGHT—A case to carry dead batteries in.

FLOOD—A river too big for its bridges.

FRECKLES—A nice suntan if you could just get them together.

FASHION—What goes out of style as soon as most people have it.

FILING CABINET—A metal box where you can systematically lose things.

FLIRT—The girl who got the boy you wanted.

GIRDLE—Device that women use to make a waist out of their waste.

GOSSIP—Someone who pumps to the conclusion.

GRANDPARENTS—Grandchild's press secretary.

HAY—Grass a la mowed.

HIGH HEELS—The invention of a girl who had been kissed on the forehead too many times.

HONEYMOON SANDWICH—Just lettuce alone.

HOWLING SUCCESS—The baby that always gets picked up.

HENPECKED HUSBAND—One who wishes Adam had died with all his ribs in his body.

HARD WORK—The accumulation of easy tasks you didn't do when you should have.

HELICOPTER—An eggbeater with enterprise.

HOBBY—What you wouldn't do for a living.

HONEYMOON—Thrill of a wifetime.

HUG—Energy gone to waist.

HUSBAND—The one who stands by you in problems you would not have had if you hadn't married him.

IGLOO—An icicle built for two.

INFLATION—A drop in the buck.

JEEP—Man's effort to make a mechanical mule.

JUNK—Something you keep for years and throw away just days before you need it.

JUVENILE DELINQUENTS—Somebody else's kids.

KISS—The way to shorten being single.

KNICKERBOCKERS—Long name for short pants.

LIFE INSURANCE—The thing that keeps you poor all your life so you can die rich.

MARRIAGE PROPOSAL—A speech usually made on the purr of the moment.

MIDDLE AGE—The time in your life when you say you are going to begin saving next month.

MILLIONAIRE—A billionaire after his taxes are paid.

MOTHER-IN-LAW—That woman who is never outspoken.

OLD-TIMER—One who can remember when a "bureau" was a piece of furniture.

OPTIMIST—He who thinks a housefly is looking for the way out.

PARKING SPACE—Unoccupied space on the other side of the street.

PATIENCE—That which is most often needed just as it is run out of.

PEDESTRIAN—The wife who counted on her husband to fill the car up with gas

POLITICS—A career that is mostly promising.

RADICAL—A person whose opinion is different from ours.

RAISIN—Grape that has seen better days.

RUSH HOUR—When traffic stands still.

SCREEN DOOR—What kids get a bang out of.

SUCCESS—When other people envy you.

SUNBURN—Getting what you basked for.

SWEATER—What a child must wear when his mother is cold.

TACT—What you think but don't say.

TIME SAVER—Love at first sight.

TOUPEE—Top secret.

ULCER—Something you get when you mountain climb over mole hills.

VACATION—A time when people find out where to stay away from next year.

WIFE—Dish jockey.

WILLPOWER—Ability to eat just one piece of chocolate.

YOUTH—The first forty years of your life and the first twenty of someone else's.

Doctor

A patient went to a doctor for a checkup. The doctor wrote out a prescription for him in his usual illegible writing. The patient put it in his pocket, but he didn't have it filled. Every morning for two years he showed it to the conductor as a railroad pass. Twice it got him into Radio City Music Hall, once into the baseball park, and once into the symphony. He got a raise from the cashier by showing it as a note from the boss. One day he mislaid it at home. His daughter picked it up, played it on the piano, and won a scholarship to a conservatory of music.

An old doctor in a small town finally took a vacation. He left his son, who was about to graduate from medical school, in charge of his practice. When the father returned, he asked his son if anything unusual had happened while he was gone.

"I cured Mrs. Stephenson of that indigestion she has been suffering from for the past thirty years," the son remarked proudly.

"Oh, no," the father exclaimed, "that indigestion has put you through high school, college, and medical school!"

Mr. Smith only visits his dentist twice a year, once for each tooth.

Patient: "Doctor, my ear rings all the time. What do you suggest?"

Doctor: "Get an unlisted ear."

Doctor: "Well, I see you're coughing easier today."
Patient: "I should be. I was awake all night practicing."

Doctor: "If I find an operation necessary, will you have the money to pay for it?"
Patient: "If I don't have the money to pay for it, will you still find the operation necessary?"

A medical student was called to the dean's office and was told, "You're doing pretty well here at school, but you will need to learn to write a little less clearly."

Patient: "Oh, Doctor, I feel so bad I want to kill myself."
Doctor: "Now, now. Just leave that to me."

Doctor: "Now look—don't you know that my office hours are from nine to five?"
Patient: "Yes, but the dog who bit me didn't."

Doctor Cooper: "You say you performed the operation just in the nick of time?"
Doctor Mosley: "Yes, in another twenty-four hours he would have recovered."

Two surgeons were wheeling a patient into the operating room. The man on the cart was under sedation but still conscious enough to hear one of the doctors say to the other, "I want you to understand that I thoroughly disagree with your diagnosis." Then the surgeon added emphatically, "And furthermore, the autopsy will prove that I am right."

A doctor told his patient there was nothing the matter with him. "All you need is more outdoor life; you must walk two or three miles regularly every day. What kind of work do you do?"

The patient replied, "I'm a postman."

Doctor: "Did you tell that boyfriend of yours what I thought of him?"

Daughter: "Yes, Father, and he said you were wrong in your diagnosis, as usual."

Two convalescents were visiting with the patient who had just been wheeled out of the operating room. "You'll be all right, don't worry," said one of the men reassuringly. "He fixed me up in good shape, and I would have been back to work by now if they hadn't opened me up again to take out a small sponge they left in me."

"I had something of a setback, too," said the other. "They had to open me up again and recover a pair of forceps dropped in my interior."

At that moment the surgeon emerged from the operating room and asked, "Has anyone seen my hat?"

Doctor: "It looks like you are a little run-down. I would suggest that you lay off golf for awhile and get a good day in at the office every now and then."

Doctor: "I think you ought to take up golf for your health."

Patient: "But Doc, I do play golf."

Doctor: "Well, in that case, maybe you'd better quit."

"My doctor says I can't play golf."

"Did he see you at his office?"

"No, he saw me out on the golf course."

"Doctor, our baby got into my golf bag and swallowed all my tees."

"Oh, I'll be right there. What are you going to do in the meantime?"

"I'm practicing my putting."

Our doctor would never operate unless it was necessary. He was just that way. If he didn't need the money, he would not lay a hand on you.

Patient (in doctor's office): "Are all these people ahead of me?"

Receptionist: "Yes, but you can go on in."

Patient: "That's OK. I've got lots of time."

Receptionist: "No you don't—I've seen your x-rays."

Doc: "You have nothing to worry about. You'll live to be sixty."

Orville: "I am sixty."

Doc: "What did I tell you?"

I've got the best doctor—if he can't cure you he will touch up the X-rays!

Where there is life there is hope—for one more medical bill.

Freda: "Doctor, Doctor, please come over quick. My dog swallowed a fountain pen!"

Doctor: "I'll be right there. But what are you doing in the meantime?"

Freda: "I'm using a pencil."

Driving

A heavyset man was hit by a person driving a Volkswagen. "Why didn't you try to go around me?" asked the man as he was being carried off on a stretcher.

"I didn't know if I had enough gas," answered the bewildered driver.

Mother: "What did you see when you went for a drive with Daddy?"

Daughter: "Lots of 'idiots' and quite a few 'hollow heads.'"

Several people were watching as a wrecker tried to loosen a foreign car that was tangled around a telephone pole. Said one observer to another, "That's the way the Mercedes Benz."

A motorist drove into a gas station and asked for ten dollars worth of gas. Efficiently, three attendants hopped to work—cleaning the windshield, checking his tires, and so on. The motorist paid his bill and left.

Several minutes later he returned and asked, "Did any of you put the gas in my car?" The three attendants huddled together, then confessed nobody had.

A minister was driving into a town one evening listening to his CB. A vulgar talking CB'er was going through town trying to make contact with a woman of ill repute.

Finally, in desperation, the caller said, "Well, I guess she doesn't have her ears on, so I'll sign off for now. Hope I catch her the next time I'm through. Sorry she couldn't hear me."

The minister picked up his CB mike and said, "She may not have heard you, but God certainly did."

There was a long silence and a voice came back on the line, "I knew this CB had a good range, but I didn't know it was that good."

"Hello! What's new? Did you hurt your hand?"
"Yes, reckless driving."
"Oh, a car."
"No, a nail."

Egotists

Father: "Now, Son, I've told you the story of your daddy and the great war."
Son: "But Daddy, what did they need all the other soldiers for?"

The young man had just graduated from college and went to work at his father's store. The first day his father asked him to sweep the floor.

"But, Dad," the son protested, "I'm a college graduate."

Replied the father, "I forgot. But don't worry, I'll show you how."

About the only good thing about egotists is they never talk about others.

Young girl to pastor: "I'm afraid I've committed the sin of vanity."
Pastor: "Why do you think that?"
Young girl: "Every time I look in the mirror I think how beautiful I look."
Pastor: "Don't worry—that isn't a sin. It's only a mistake."

Librarian: "You must be quiet. The girl next to you can't read."
Bob: "That's terrible. I started reading when I was five."

Success turned his head. It's too bad it didn't wring his neck a little.

You can't get anywhere with Harry by shaking his hand when he puts it out—you need to kiss it.

Ever since he became a self-made man, he began a lifelong romance.

You'd be a millionaire if you could buy Greg for what you think of him and sell him for what he thinks of himself.

He's so conceited he takes a bow when he hears thunder.

Someday he will learn that it is only nineteen inches between a pat on the back and a kick in the pants.

An after-dinner speaker was rushed to the hospital and an inexperienced nurse was assigned to him. She put a barometer in his mouth instead of a thermometer and it read, "dry and windy."

"Beth, you are a very, very vain little girl," exclaimed her mother. "You are always looking at yourself in the mirror. You don't see me looking in the mirror all the time, do you?"

"No, Mother, I don't," admitted Beth. "But you don't have to—you can see me without looking in the mirror."

A rather arrogant churchman was trying to impress upon the young minds of a class of boys and girls the importance of leading a Christian life. "Why do people call me a Christian, children?" the worthy man asked, standing very erect and smiling down at them.

After a pause a shrill little voice said, "Because they don't know you?"

Sailor: "Tease me if you like, but I'll bet that in ten minutes after we hit port I'll be walking down the street with a beautiful woman on each arm."

Marine: "Shucks! There never was a tattoo artist who could work that fast!"

If people listened to themselves more often, they would probably talk less.

She thinks she is a siren, but she looks more like a false alarm.

He has an alarm clock and a telephone that don't ring—they applaud.

He's never been known to say a mean thing about anyone—that's because he only talks about himself.

He's going through life with his horn stuck.

Success has not only gone to her head but to her mouth also.

He's so stuck on himself he even signs his name to anonymous letters.

He has a mirror on his bathroom ceiling so he can see himself gargle.

Her greatest admirer is her husband's wife.

He won't admit he's conceited. He just happens to have a high opinion of people with ability, charm, good looks, and personality.

If I want your opinion, I'll give it to you!

I might not agree with what you say, but I'll punch you in the mouth if you say it!

"Dr. Jekyll, tell me about your alter ego."
"No. You are getting under my Hyde."

Farming

Fred: "How's your father's dairy farm doing?"
Don: "Great. He's training all the cows to sleep on their backs."
Fred: "What for?"
Don: "So in the morning the cream will be on top."

Three preachers were enjoying a chicken dinner at the home of one of their members. After the meal the farmer took them to the barn. There was one rooster with his head held quite high. One minister remarked to another, "That's a pretty cocky rooster."

The farmer replied, "You would be cocky too, if you had three sons who just entered the ministry!"

A farmer's helper was running a reaper and binder. He fell off and the machine ran over him, with one of the sharp blades cutting off his nose. He quickly picked up his severed nose and stuck it back on, fastening it with a bandage so that it would grow back on. After it had time to heal, he took the bandage off and found his nose had grown back on. However, in his excitement he had put it on upside down! Even at that, he decided he could get along. Only every time it rained it strangled him, and whenever he sneezed he blew his hat off.

Unable to restrain his curiosity, a stranger asked a farmer what the reason was for the strange behavior of his hogs. The farmer explained in a husky voice, "It's like this. I used to call the hogs at feeding time, but my voice failed so that I could no longer holler loud enough, so then I started knocking on that old hollow log. Now these darned woodpeckers are about to run them to death."

A farmer's mule kicked his mother-in-law in the head and she died. A large crowd gathered for the funeral, most of them men. Following the service the minister said, "Mrs. Bailey must have been a very popular lady. Just look at all the people who have stopped their chores to come to her funeral."

"They aren't here for the funeral, pastor," commented one old farmer. "They're here to bid on the mule."

A city boy and country boy were walking down the street. Coming toward them was a product of the beauty parlor just down the street—permanent wave, bright fingernails, drugstore complexion and flashy lipstick.

"What do you think of that?" asked the city boy.

The country boy looked carefully and replied, "Speaking as a farmer, I'd say that must have been some pretty poor soil to require so much topdressing."

The successful farmer vowed he increased egg production by hanging this sign in his hen house: "An egg a day keeps Colonel Sanders away."

Farmer (carrying a milk pail and approaching a cow): "Well, Elsie, what will it be today—milk or chopped steak?"

A new bride went to the grocery store to do her weekly shopping. She was determined that the grocer not comment on her youth and inexperience. "These eggs are awfully small," she criticized. "I know it," answered the grocer, "but that's the kind the farmer brings me. They are fresh from the country this morning." "Well, that's the trouble with those farmers," said the bride, "they are so anxious to get their eggs sold that they take them off the nest too soon."

A farmer went into a hotel, and the clerk asked him if he wanted to register. The farmer said, "No, I don't expect to vote here."

A visitor to a farm asked the farmer's son where his father could be found. "He's down at the end of the lot feeding the pigs," replied the boy. "You'll recognize Father. He has a hat on."

Have you heard the one about the farmer who walked into a dealer's showroom with a shoebox full of hundred dollar bills and tried to buy a tractor? The salesman could tell him the monthly payments, but he didn't know the price in cash. The bookkeeper quit because she didn't know how to record the transaction, and the sales manager canceled the sale because he didn't have a credit report.

He lies so much that when he wants his pigs to come and eat he has to get someone else to call them for him.

Forgetfulness

Husband to wife: "How can you expect me to remember your birthday—you never look any older!"

Did you hear about the absentminded professor who returned from lunch and saw a sign on his door, "Back in fifteen minutes," then sat down to wait for himself? Slammed his wife and kissed the door? Got up and lit a match to see if he had blown out the candle?

"You're charged with being disorderly," charged the judge. "Have you anything to say?"

"Conscience doth make cowards of us all," intoned the prisoner. "I'm not as depraved as Fitzgerald, as dissolute as Kipling, as ungrateful as Hemingway, as demented as Galsworthy, or as tasteless as Shakespeare . . ."

"That's enough," interrupted the judge, "ten days. Bailiff, make a list of the names he mentioned and 'round 'em all up."

A preacher was trying to patch up a difference between two friends. "You must not cherish enmity against your neighbor," he said to the one who was complaining. "If your neighbor does you harm you must forget it."

"I do forget it, but I have such a bad memory that I keep forgetting that I forget."

He has three pairs of glasses: one for nearsightedness, one for farsightedness, and a third pair to look for the other two.

An antique dealer was passing through a small village and stopped to watch an old man chopping wood with what appeared to be a very ancient ax.

"That's a mighty, mighty old ax you're swinging there," observed the dealer.

"Yep," said the old man, "mighty old. Matter of fact, it once belonged to Sir Walter Raleigh!"

"Not really!" ventured the dealer. "Well, all I can say is, it sure is well preserved."

"Of course," admitted the old man, "its handle has been replaced four or five times and its head twenty times."

"I've changed my mind!" he snapped.

"Does it work any better?"

The sales manager was talking to his secretary. "Our city salesman, Steve, sure is absentminded. He can't remember a thing. I sent him out for a pack of cigarettes for me. I'll bet he'll forget to come back at all."

About that time Steve came in. "Sir, you'll never guess what happened to me about an hour ago. I stopped in to see that old grouch at the Ace Company who has never bought anything from us, and I sold him a $6,000 order."

The sales manager threw up his hands in disgust.

"See there! I told you he'd forget the cigarettes."

A motivational expert opened his sales talk to the production manager.

"I would like to talk to your employees and show them how my new motivational course can put a sparkle and fire into their work," he said.

"Get out of here! Don't you know this is a dynamite factory?" roared the production manager.

One time he was in a fight—and was knocked conscious.

Theo: "Doc, you have got to help me. I think I'm losing my mind. I can't remember anything."
Doc: "When did you first realize this problem?"
Theo: "What problem?"

Grandparents

For two solid hours, the lady sitting next to a man on an airplane had told him about her grandchildren. She had even produced a plastic foldout photograph album of all eight of her grandchildren.

After talking for two hours about the grandchildren, she finally realized that she had dominated the whole conversation.

"Oh, I've done all the talking, and I'm so sorry. I know you certainly have something to say. Please, tell me—what do *you* think of my grandchildren?"

Grandpa: "Have I told you about my grandchildren?"
Friend: "No—and I certainly do appreciate it."

Satisfied grandmother: "If I had to do it all over again—I'd just bypass children and have grandchildren!"

A young girl was examining her grandmother's wedding ring. "Wow, what heavy and awkward rings they made fifty years ago!" commented the young girl.

"That is true," replied the grandmother, "but in my day they were made to last a lifetime!"

Little Tracey accidentally knocked over a vase and it broke. A friend said, "Won't you get in trouble for breaking that vase?"

"Ah, no," answered Tracey, "I won't get in trouble—my grandma lives with us."

"Amy, every time you are bad I get another gray hair."
"Golly!" replied Amy, "You must have been a terror. Just look at grandma!"

Grandfather (at the zoo): "Cathy, don't be frightened. The tiger is going to be fed and that is what makes him roar so loud."
Cathy: "Oh, I'm not afraid. Daddy goes on just like that when his supper isn't ready."

Little Scottie: "Grandpa, will Daddy be an angel? He's got whiskers, and angels don't have any."
Grandpa: "Well, your father may get there, but it will be a close shave."

Home

There were guests in the home of five-year-old Christy. All evening long she wore her best company manners. But the moment the door closed behind them she became disobedient.
Her mother asked, "Why is it that you are being so naughty now? You were such a lovely little girl while our guests were here."
"Why, Mother," answered Christy, "you don't use your company silver all the time, do you?"

"To get my son out of bed in the morning, I just open his door and toss the cat on his bed," explained a resourceful mother.
"He sleeps with his dog."

The only thing some kids and their parents will communicate to each other is a bad cold.

The little boy went home from Sunday School and told his mother about Moses and the Red Sea crossing.

"Moses got behind the enemy lines," the lad said, "and he had his engineers build a pontoon bridge across the Red Sea. Moses' people crossed over. When his spies told him a corps of Egyptian tanks was about to cross the bridge, he got on his walkie-talkie and ordered his air force to blow up the bridge. The air force blew it up and the Israelites were saved."

"Are you sure that's the story the Sunday School teacher told you?" the mother asked.

"No," said the boy, "but you just wouldn't believe the way the teacher told it!"

Husband to wife as they leave baby-sitter with young son and start out for the evening: "I still say that when they begin asking for a blonde instead of a brunette, they are old enough to stay alone!"

"Where does the good Lord live?" asked the Sunday School teacher of a little four-year-old boy in her class.

"In our bathroom," replied the youngster.

"What makes you think so?" inquired the curious teacher.

"Because," answered the boy, "every morning I hear my father shout, 'Good Lord, are you still in there!'"

"I'm old enough to get an allowance," a young daughter said to her father. The father agreed to give his daughter a weekly allowance if she would keep accurate records of the way she spent her money.

"At the end of each month," he said, "I would like to see a written account of how much you have spent of your allowance."

At the end of the first month, the father was delighted to see that his daughter had kept fairly good records. She had indicated the amount of money given to the ministries of her church as well as money spent on clothes, books, club dues, recreation, and savings. The last item was labeled "T.L.O.K." The sum amounted to nearly one-fifth of the total amount she had spent.

"What in the world is T.L.O.K.?" he asked.

"Well," said the daughter. "It's this way. Sometimes I did not jot down the sums I spent. When I sat down to try to make out my account, I could not for the life of me remember where I had spent all my money. I could not make my accounts balance so I had to place several dollars under T.L.O.K."

"But what does it mean?" asked her father.

The daughter replied, "T.L.O.K. means The Lord Only Knows."

The best way for the typical American family to get to know one another better is for the TV set to break down.

Wife during argument: "OK, I'll meet you halfway. I will admit I'm right if you'll admit you are wrong."

A husband and wife were having an argument about who was the most extravagant.

"You accuse me of reckless extravagance," he said. "When did I ever make a useless expenditure?"

She replied, "Well, that fire extinguisher you bought several months ago—we never used it, not even once!"

Mike and Jeff were helping move furniture. Mike was sweating, carrying a dresser uphill, when his dad called out, "I thought Jeff was helping you move that!"

"He is," explained Mike, "he's inside carrying the clothes hangers."

Instead of going to school one day a young boy went fishing. On his way home he met some friends coming home from school. When they saw he was carrying a fishing pole they asked, "Catch anything?"

Replied the boy, "Not yet. I ain't been home."

Wife: "The maid has stolen two of our towels!"
Husband: "Which towels were they?"
Wife: "The ones we brought back from the hotel in Denver!"

Boss: "How long will you be off on your honeymoon?"
Employee: "Well, how long do you suggest?"
Boss: "I don't know. I haven't seen the bride."

New bride: "Honey, let's pretend that we have been married for a long time."
Groom: "All right. But do you think you can carry all those suitcases?"

Lynn: "We passed right by your house yesterday."
Kelly: "Thanks. We really appreciate it."

An explosion in the kitchen sent a man and his wife hurtling out the window and into the neighbor's yard. Later, the neighbor said, "It was the first time this couple had gone out together since they have been married."

A wise mother had her son learn how to be a caddy, so that he might occasionally run into his father.

After all is said and done, it is she who has said it and he who has done it.

When they have a disagreement they soon patch things up—like his nose, his jaw, and his head.

Marriage for him is like a railroad sign—when he first met her, he stopped, then he looked, now he listens.

He mumbled as he sat at the dinner table, "How quiet it must have been in the Tower of Babel!"

A man's home is his hassle.

Insults

NICKNAMES

ACCORDIONIST—He plays both ends against the middle.

BUSINESSWOMAN—She's interested in everybody's business.

BUTTON—He's always popping off at the wrong time.

CLASS CONSCIOUS—He has no class, and everyone is conscious of it.

CLIFF—He is a big bluff.

CONVERTIBLE TOP—She has been a blonde, a brunette, and a redhead.

COOKIE—He has such a crummy look.

CORN—In school he was always at the foot of the class.

DON JUAN—The girls "Don Juan" to have anything to do with him.

DRIP—You can hear him, but you can't turn him off.

FISH—He gets into trouble because he can't keep his mouth shut.

GOAT—He's always butting in.

LILAC—She can lilac anything.

MIRACLE WORKER—It's a miracle when he works.

MYTH—He's a myth-fit.

PIE—He has lots of crust.

RIVER—The biggest part of him is his mouth.

THEORY—He hardly ever works.

WHEELBARROW—He needs to be pushed.

INSULTING REMARKS

I can't really blame you for your ancestors, but I sure must blame them for you.

Let's play Building and Loan. Just get out of the building and leave me alone.

If Moses had known anyone like you, there would have been another Commandment.

You could make a decent living hiring yourself out to scare people with the hiccups.

Look, I'm not going to engage in a battle of wits with you—I never attack anyone who is not armed.

You make me wish I had a lower IQ so I could enjoy your company.

Tell me, is that your lower lip or are you wearing a turtleneck sweater?

It's not the ups and downs of life that get to me—it's the jerks like you.

I'll bet you are called a big thinker—by people who lisp.

A crumb like you should have stayed in bread.

I understand when you were a kid your mother sent your picture to Ripley and it was returned, marked, "I don't believe it!"

Why don't you go and have your jocular vein cut?

The longer I know you, the more I depreciate you.

Anytime you happen to pass my house, I'll appreciate it.

You may be a tonic to your family, but to me you are a pill.

The defense lawyer in a robbery case was cross-examining a witness.

"When did the robbery take place?" demanded the lawyer.

"I think . . ." began the witness.

"We don't care what you think, Sir," the lawyer interrupted. "We want to know what you know."

"Then if you don't want to know what I think," said the witness, "I might as well leave the stand; I can't talk without thinking—I'm not a lawyer."

I wouldn't say my father-in-law is stupid, but he does have "T.G.I.F." on his slippers—"Toes Go In First."

Jealousy

Wife: "Did you see that fur coat Mrs. Myers wore to church today?"

Husband: "No, I didn't."

Wife: "Did you see that hat Mrs. Brown wore to church?"

Husband: "No, I didn't."

Wife: "Well, it doesn't do you much good to go to church!"

Marsha was very jealous when she heard that her most recent boyfriend had asked Lisa to marry him. She happened to run into Lisa at the shopping mall and said, "So, I've heard that you've accepted Allen's marriage proposal. Did he ever tell you that he once proposed to me?"

"Why, no," answered Allen's fiancée. "He did tell me once

that there were several things in his life he was very ashamed of, but I didn't ask him what they were."

BORN EXECUTIVE: Someone whose father owns the business.

"I'm Mr. Wilson's wife," said a brunette, introducing herself to a pretty blonde at a party.
Said the blonde, "Oh, I'm his secretary."
Wryly, the wife said, "Oh, *were* you?"

"If your mother gave you a large apple and a small one and told you to divide with your brother, which apple would you keep?"
"Do you mean my big brother or my little brother?"

Jobs

Personnel manager: "We are looking for a responsible person to fill this job."
Applicant: "Well, I'm the right person for this job. Of all the jobs I've ever had, if something went wrong, I was responsible."

There was an undertaker who signed all his correspondence, "Eventually yours."

The young high school graduate applied for his first job in a local machine shop. He filled out the application and came to a question that asked, "What machines can you operate?"
The young man thought for a long time and wrote, "Pac Man and Donkey Kong."

A man applying for a job asked the manager, "How many people work in this plant?"

"Oh," the manager replied, "about one in fifteen."

Personnel manager: "So you would like a job in this office? Well, what can you do?"

Prospective employee: "Nothing."

Personnel manager: "Sorry, but you should have applied sooner. All those high-paying jobs are filled."

A wealthy woman was interviewing an applicant for a job on her household staff.

"Do you know how to serve company?" she asked.

"Yes ma'am, both ways," replied the young girl.

"And what do you mean by 'both ways'?"

"Why, so they will come back and so they won't."

A young girl applied for a job as a secretary and was given a spelling test.

"How do you spell Mississippi?" she was asked.

"The state or the river?"

Have you heard about the politician who's thinking of running for show business?

A man was applying for a job and asked the personnel manager, "Does your company pay for Blue Cross insurance?"

"No, you pay for it. It is deducted from your salary each month," answered the personnel manager.

"Well, the last place I worked they paid for it," commented the applicant.

"Did they provide you with a life insurance policy?"

"Yes."

"And profit sharing?"

"Yes."

"Paid vacations?"

"Sure, and they gave bonuses, and gifts, and. . . ."

"Well, why did you leave the company?"

"They folded."

Personnel manager: "Why were you discharged by your last employer?"

Applicant: "I was too ambitious."

Personnel manager: "Why did you leave your last job?"

Applicant: "Sickness. The boss got sick of me."

The father came home exhausted, hoping to get some rest. But little Bobby kept asking questions.

"What do you do all day at your job, Daddy?"

"Nothing!" shouted the father.

After a long pause, Bobby finally asked, "Daddy, how do you know when you are through?"

Success always occurs in private. Failure always occurs in full view of the public.

He has so many yes men working for him, his company is called "the Land of Nod."

He's well-known as a miracle worker—it's a miracle when he is working.

She works eight hours and sleeps eight hours—her boss is firing her because they are the same eight hours.

80

Mike and Will were chatting about their teenagers.

"What's your boy going to do for a living?" asked Will.

"I'm going to let him be a lawyer," said Mike. "He is always putting his nose into other people's business, so he might as well get paid for it."

Bar Association's Theme Song: "Sweet Sue."

Did you hear about the lawyer who was so successful that he had his own ambulance?

LAWYER: A guy who is willing to spend your last cent to prove he is right.

Patron (in shoe repair shop): "I found this ticket from 1977. I don't reckon you still have them."

Cobbler: "They'll be ready on Friday."

Ron: "Why do some of our canine friends prefer to stay at home?"

Art: "Because it's a dog-eat-dog world out there!"

First mailman: "A dog bit me on the leg yesterday."

Second mailman: "Did you put anything on it?"

First mailman: "No, he liked it plain!"

Overheard: "The pup was here. The pup will be here. The pup is not here."

Remark: "He's going into the army and he heard you have to use pup tense!"

Mannerisms

The six-year-old went to school looking very grown up in a new dress and shoes. When she came home her mother asked if anyone had mentioned her new clothes.

"Yes," she replied, "the teacher did. She said as long as I dressed like a lady, why didn't I act like one?"

Chairman of the board to personnel director—"Who did you get to fill Charlie's vacancy?"

Answer—"Charlie didn't leave a vacancy."

A college professor stopped to talk to one of his students. He asked, "Which way was I going when I stopped to talk to you?"

"That way," the student pointed.

"Good," the professor said, "then I've had lunch."

"One night I dreamed I ate a five-pound marshmallow, and the next morning my pillow was gone."

"He was the only person Dale Carnegie ever punched in the nose."

"Will Rogers never met him."

I know a congressman who is so unpopular that one year he ran unopposed and still lost.

Timmy had been invited to dinner at the house of some particular people, and his mother, who was not going with him, was nervous about his table manners. She gave him specific instructions before leaving home, and on his return asked him several questions.

"Oh, I did all right," Timmy assured her. "I only did one thing wrong, and I couldn't help it. But don't worry. I got out of it OK."

"What happened, Timmy?" asked his anxious mother.

"Oh, I was cutting my meat and it slipped off my plate onto the floor."

"Good heavens! What did you do?" asked his mother.

"Oh, I just carelessly said, 'That's always the way with tough meat,' and went on eating my dinner."

A man got off a plane in Hawaii and asked a bystander, "How do you natives pronounce it? Hawaii or Havaii?"

"Havaii," said the native.

"Thank you," said the traveler.

"You're velcome," replied the native.

It even takes him three hours to tell you that he's a man of few words.

No one is her equal at using more words to say less about nothing.

He considers free speech not as a right but as a continuous obligation.

She has bought dozens of books on how to speak in public. What she really needs is one on how to shut up.

He says the Constitution of the United States allows him to talk as much as he wants. The only problem is, the United States has a stronger constitution than his listeners.

He always has too much conversation left over at the end of his ideas.

Her expenditure of words is too great for her income of ideas.

He's so opinionated that one day his wife said, "Tomorrow is Tuesday, if that's all right with you."

What this country needs is a good no-scent cigar.

As ye smoke, so shall ye reek.

"Hey, Ernie. Are you wearing a hearing aid?"
"Yeah, the latest thing. Best kind ever made. It really works great. I can hear a little bird a hundred yards away. I can recognize the tinkle of a bell across the street."
"Great. You'd never know. What kind is it?"
"Half past five."

Men

He shows pictures of his children and plays a sound track of his wife.

How come a man will go from an air-conditioned house to an air-conditioned office in an air-conditioned car to a health spa and pay forty dollars an hour to sweat?

Husband: "I think the dry climate would disagree with me."
Wife: "Honey, it wouldn't dare."

Craig: "Do you know who the greatest commander in the world is?"

Dick: "Of course I do. I married her."

Joe: "Have you seen any of your childhood dreams come true?"

Jack: "Sure have. When my mother used to comb my hair I used to wish I didn't have any."

His nickname is Sanka—he has no active ingredient in the bean.

A considerate husband is one who remembers to oil the lawnmower for his wife before he goes out to play golf.

A wife pointed to her husband stretched out in a hammock and explained, "Fred's hobby is letting birds watch him."

Husband: "Is dinner ready yet?"

Wife: "No, Honey. I started it according to the time you set the clock for when you came home last night—so it won't be ready for four hours."

"Doctor, if there is something wrong with me, please don't scare me to death by using a scientific name. Just tell me what it is in plain English," said the patient.

"Well," said the doctor, "to be honest with you, you are just plain lazy."

"Thanks, doc," sighed the patient with relief, "now give me the scientific name for it so I can go home and tell my wife."

She's the power behind the drone.

Harry: "I got some new golf clubs for my wife."
Dave: "Wow, that is great! I wish I could make a trade like that."

Wife: "I know it's too much to expect, but I think if you ever spent a Saturday at home with me, instead of out on the golf course, I'd drop dead."
Husband: "Look, it's not going to do you any good to try and bribe me."

"My wife says if I don't quit golfing she will leave me."
"Man, that's too bad."
"Yeah, I will miss her."

His supervisor and his wife are both demanding to see his birth certificate for proof he's alive.

It's too much trouble for him to make coffee, so he puts coffee beans in his mustache and sips hot water.

He's one husband who could make a wife a lucky widow.

She wishes she'd paid closer attention to the sign on the courthouse steps: "This way for marriage licenses. Watch your step."

She asked her husband for some money for a rainy day so he gave her a rubber check.

He: "You don't deserve a man like me!"
She: "I don't deserve migraine headaches either, but I've got them!"

She drives from the backseat, and he cooks from the kitchen table.

They are a fastidious couple—he's fast and she's hideous.

Tina: "Finally, he's learned to communicate."
Beverly: "Well, what have you learned about him?"
Tina: "That he has nothing to say."

Misfortune

Long on egotism but short on cash, a young actor was trying to talk his landlord into waiting for the rent money.

"Just think," he said, "in a few years people will pass by this apartment and say, 'Williams, the famous actor, once lived there.'"

Said the landlord, "If I don't get my rent today they will be able to say it tomorrow."

I don't know the meaning of the word *defeat,* and thousands of other words.

I locked myself in the car and had to break one of the windows to get out.

I have turned a few heads in my day, and a few stomachs, too.

My face looks like it was used for testing golf shoes.

I talk so much I should open a branch mouth.

When I go to the zoo, the elephants throw peanuts at me.

I am on the crucial list at Weight Watchers.

I don't know what makes me so obnoxious; whatever it is, it surely works.

I was invited to a séance—and nobody would hold my hand.

Saying nice things about me is like speaking out on behalf of athlete's foot.

May a ninety-year-old garlic farmer give me mouth-to-mouth resuscitation.

May I get a vapor lock in my pacemaker.

My toupee makes me look twenty-five years sillier.

My cooking is so bad even the garbage disposal refuses it.

A young man who had not had much schooling was being examined for a preaching license. One of the questions asked of him was, "What is the difference between the seraphim and cherubim?" He thought for a while and answered, "I knew there had been a little trouble between them, but I thought it had all been cleared up."

It might have been the same fellow who thought that the "epistles were the wives of the apostles."

Another fellow, but obviously not a ministerial student, thought Easter Sunday was Billy Sunday's sister.

A new minister in town asked a young boy to show him the way to the post office. "Right this way," said the young boy as he pointed in the right direction.

"Son, if you come to my church at 7:30 this evening, I will show you the way to heaven," said the new minister.

"Shucks! You don't even know the way to the post office!"

A farmer coming into town with a load of hay heard the clang of a gong and the sound of wheels behind him. A mounted policeman galloped up and shouted, "Out of the way of the fire department!"

The farmer moved over to one side to let the fire engine pass. Then he went back into the middle of the street just in time to be hit by the hook and ladder truck. As he was crawling out of the mess, the policeman galloped up to him once more. "I warned you to get out of the way of the fire department!"

Replied the confused farmer, "I did get out of the way of the fire department, but how was I to know there were a lot of drunk painters coming along behind them?"

When all you have is a hammer, everything looks like a nail.

The best laid plans of mice and men are usually about the same.

When I was young my father lent me money to buy a rattle.

The other day I went into a store to buy a suit. I told the salesman I wanted to see something cheap, and he told me to look in the mirror.

When I was a baby they bought me a carriage that didn't have any brakes.

I played hide and seek, and they wouldn't look for me.

One time I had a fever. They put a thermometer in my mouth, and my father said, "OK, Son, bite hard."

One time I asked my mother if I could go ice skating on the neighbor's pond, and she told me to wait until it got warmer.

Once when I told my mother that nobody liked me, she said, "Don't say that. Everybody hasn't met you yet."

I never had friends at the park. I'll never forget the seesaw. I had to keep running from one end to the other.

The day I got married was really embarrassing. The minister said, "If anyone does not agree with this marriage, speak now or forever hold your peace." I turned around, and her family had formed a double line.

Husband: "I didn't get the raise I asked for, but the boss broke my arm and I'll be getting worker's compensation."

I have to go to the mountains because of respiratory trouble (my creditors won't let me breathe).

My mother died before her time (she was hanged at 10:30 instead of 10:45, as scheduled).

My father was cleaned out in the 1929 stock market crash (a broker jumped out of the window and landed on his pushcart).

The light at the end of the tunnel just might be the headlight of an oncoming train.

A bum came up to me outside the Hilton. That's where I live, outside the Hilton. He said, "I haven't eaten in five days." I said to him, "That's a shame. Force yourself."

I'll never forget the day my dad caught me smoking. Boy, did he scream at the guy who set me on fire!

I had my nose fixed—now my mouth won't work.

I spent my vacation in my own backyard. It showed my neighbors what kind of person I am—practical, home loving, and broke.

I like to go to the drive-in window at the bank—it lets my car see who its real owner is.

Our house is so dirty even the mice have athlete's foot.

Mistakes

At a fancy dinner party the hostess who was sitting at the far end of the table from a famous actress wrote a note to the actress and had the maid deliver it.

The actress couldn't read without her glasses, so she asked the man on her right to read it to her. "It says," he read, 'Darling, do me a favor and don't ignore the man on your right. I know he is a bore, but talk to him anyway.'"

Teacher: "What is a synonym?"
Young girl: "It's a word you can use in place of the one you don't know how to spell."

A class of little girls were asked the meaning of the word *philosopher.* Little Cindy raised her hand and replied, "A philosopher is a man who rides a philosopede."

Two men, thinking they knew each other, crossed the street to shake hands. On discovering their error, one cried, "I beg your pardon!"

"Oh, don't mention it, it's a mutual mistake. I thought it was you and you thought it was me, and after all it was neither of us."

Almost anything is easier to get into than it is to get out of.

All inanimate objects can move about enough to get in your way.

When a problem goes away, the people trying to solve it don't.

The following note was placed on an order for an engraving of a plaque: "This is a special anniversary gift . . . please spell the name *write*."

Sign advertising the book of the month: "*Let's Praise the Lord* this month only."

Robby's Sunday School class was listening to the story of Lot's wife looking back and turning into a pillar of salt. "One time my mommy was driving and when she looked back she turned into a telephone pole," commented little Robby.

Mr. Bishop noticed a very ugly woman sitting across the room. "Who in the world is that extremely homely woman over there?"

"That," answered Mr. Moore, "is my wife."

Quite embarrassed, Mr. Bishop promptly replied, "Well, you ought to see mine."

A young man was very much in love with a beautiful young girl. One day she told him that the next day was her birthday. He told her he would send her a bouquet of roses, one for each year of her life.

That evening he called the florist and ordered twenty-five roses and instructed that they be delivered first thing the next morning.

The next morning as the florist was preparing the order he decided that since the young man was such a good customer he would put an extra dozen roses in the bouquet.

The young man never did find out what made the young girl so angry with him.

Architects cover their mistakes with ivy, doctors with sod, artists with paint, and brides with mayonnaise.

To err is human, but it takes a computer to really mess things up.

A newcomer applied for a job in a power plant.

"What can you do?" asked the chief.

"Anything, Sir, just anything," replied the applicant.

"Well," drawled the chief, thinking to have some fun, "you seem to be all right. Could you wheel out a barrow of smoke?"

"Sure," he exclaimed. "Just fill it up for me."

Have you seen the new pencils with erasers on both ends? They are made especially for people who do nothing but make mistakes.

A teenager was driving his car down a one-way street, the wrong way.

"Where do you think you're going?" asked the policeman.

"I don't know, but I must be late, 'cause everybody is coming back."

A young man said to a lady, "Your stockings are wrinkled." The lady said, "Shut up. I don't have any stockings on."

Young girl (on first fishing trip): "How much did that red and white thing cost?"

Boyfriend: "Oh, you mean that float? About twenty-five cents."

Young girl: "Well, I guess I owe you twenty-five cents. Mine just sank."

Woman (to cook): "Mary, when you serve the dinner for my guests this evening, don't spill anything."

Cook: "Don't worry, ma'am. I never talk much."

A long-winded preacher was shaking hands with some of the members of his congregation. One of his members was a little confused and kept calling him "neverend" instead of "reverend."

"The boy who had made good" was returning to visit his old hometown, and the citizens were anxious to honor him. However, he was rather puffed up over his success and gave the impression there was nothing he didn't know.

The chairman of the committee said to him, "Bob, just one little sad note in all this music of your reception and I hope you will speak of it in your speech tonight. One of our most beloved citizens died yesterday—old Dr. Bellows—do you remember him?" The speaker lied, of course, and said, yes, he remembered him very well. He made a note on his manuscript and launched into a eulogy of "Dear, old Dr. Bellows—he meant so much to me and my family. He helped bring me into this world."

At this point the chairman jerked on his coattail and whispered, "Hush, you fool. Dr. Bellows was a veterinarian."

The prisoner was being questioned by the judge. "Do you deny that you stole this typewriter?"

Cried the prisoner, "Gee! Is that a typewriter? I thought it was a cash register!"

A city farmer tied his cow's tail to his leg while he was milking. Afterwards he said that he had not gone around the barn more than eight times until he knew he had made a mistake.

Murphy's Law was not invented by Murphy but by another man with the same name.

Two wrongs are only the beginning.

Nothing is as inevitable as a mistake whose time has come.

Where there is a will, there is a won't.

Once you open a can of worms, the only way you can recan them is to use a bigger can.

Never open a can of worms unless you plan to go fishing.

There is no job so easy that it can't be done wrong.

A flying particle will find the nearest eye.

Mothers-in-Law

The first time my mother-in-law came to our house, I said, "Ma, make my home your home." She did—she sold it!

A retired banker decided to go on a safari to Africa. He asked his wife to accompany him. She said she would only if she could bring her mother along. Having suffered his mother-in-law for thirty-five years, the banker was grieved but finally agreed.

In Kenya they hired a famous hunter and made their way to the bush. One morning when they were in gorilla country the banker discovered that his mother-in-law was missing. He and his wife called for their guide. Together they followed the tracks into the dense jungle. Suddenly they heard a noise and through a clearing saw a giant gorilla, with Mama slung over his shoulder, entering a cave.

"What shall we do?" cried the banker's wife. "What shall we do?"

"Nothing," said the banker. "Absolutely nothing. That stupid gorilla got himself into this mess. Now let him get out of it."

Vet: "You will ruin this dog's looks if you have his tail cut off. Why are you insisting on it?"

Husband: "My mother-in-law is coming for a visit and I want to eliminate any possible signs of welcome."

Interior decorator—Someone who tells you what kind of furniture to buy, what kind of drapes to hang, what colors to use around your house—sort of like a mother-in-law with a license.

Ad in newspaper: "I received a threatening letter today from a man who said if I didn't send him $5,000 he'd kidnap my mother-in-law. Well, if that man is reading this, I want to tell him I don't have that kind of money. But I'm interested in his proposition."

Man on city bus: "I don't have anything to worry about. My wife takes care of the money, and my mother-in-law takes care of my business. All I need to do is work."

Customer: "You made a mistake on this prescription for my mother-in-law. Instead of quinine, you used strychnine."

Pharmacist: "Really! I guess you owe me one dollar more."

A mother-in-law was visiting her daughter. Her son-in-law came home in a state of shock.

"Mom," he cried, "there are eight men outside with vacuum cleaners, and they all claim they have an appointment for a demonstration!"

"That's right," the mother-in-law replied. "Now you just show them all to different rooms and let them start demonstrating."

She: "I should have taken my mother's advice and never married you! Oh, how she tried to stop me!"

He: "Good grief! How I've misjudged that woman!"

His daughter, reluctant to accept a marriage proposal, said, "Dad, I hate to leave Mom."

"That's OK," he said, "take her with you."

Judge: "You are charged with pushing your mother-in-law out the window of her twenty-eighth-floor apartment."

Prisoner: "I did it without thinking, sir."

Judge: "Yes, but don't you see how dangerous it might have been for anyone passing at the time?"

Old Age

Middle age is when the narrow waist and the broad mind change places.

He: "Did you see how pleased Mrs. Smith looked when I told her she didn't look a day older than her daughter?"

She: "I didn't notice. I was too busy watching the expression on her daughter's face."

You know you're getting older when . . .

. . . your little black book contains only names ending in M.D.

. . . you decide to procrastinate and never get around to it.

. . . you look forward to a dull evening.

. . . you walk with your head held high, trying to get used to your bifocals.

. . . you sit in a rocking chair and can't get it going.

. . . your knees buckle and your belt won't.

. . . dialing long distance wears you out.

. . . you burn the midnight oil after 9:00 PM.

. . . your back goes out more than you do.

. . . you sink your teeth into a steak and they stay there.

One couple got married so late in life that Medicare paid for their honeymoon.

You know you're getting old when your work is less fun and your fun is more work.

A nice old gentleman of seventy-five got a good report from his doctor after his medical examination, and the doctor asked him how he kept in such good shape.

"Well, Sir," he explained, "when I got married about fifty years ago, my wife and I made an agreement that if I lost my temper she would stay silent and if she lost her temper I would leave the house. I credit my good health to the well-known advantages of an outdoor life."

Ted: "Your wife used to be terribly nervous. Now she is very calm and collected. What happened?"

Mike: "The doctor told her that nervousness was a usual symptom of advancing age."

Trim figures: What some people do when they tell their ages.

At a party for an ice-skating queen, a woman said to her husband, "My, she certainly looks young."

"Why shouldn't she?" answered the husband. "She's been on ice all of her life."

An elderly man invested in a hearing aid that was virtually invisible and was assured by the salesman that he could return it if it didn't prove twice as effective as the large hearing aid he had been using for several years. He returned to the store in a few days to tell the clerk of his satisfaction with his new hearing aid.

"I'll bet your family likes it too," commented the salesclerk.

"Oh, they don't know about it," said the elderly gentleman. "And boy, am I having a great time with it! I've changed my will three times in the last two days!"

Pushing sixty is not exercise enough.

The formula for being forever young will work once they iron out a few wrinkles.

"A person born in 1932 is how old today?"

"A man or woman?"

I was going to get a face-lift, but when I found out how much it cost, I let the whole thing drop.

"Sir," said the usher at the theater, "you musn't be poking around people's feet like that."

"But, I've lost my gum," said the man as he continued to prowl around under the seat.

"Why, that's not important enough to disturb everyone," declared the usher.

"I'm afraid you don't understand," explained the man, "my false teeth are in that gum!"

"I'm going to marry a twenty-five-year-old girl," said the eighty-year-old man to his doctor, who was giving him a complete physical exam.

"That could be fatal," answered the physician.

"Well, so be it," replied the old man. "If she dies, she dies."

Patience

After a day of complete harassment, the mother shook her finger at her small, unruly youngster.

"All right, Junior," she shouted, "do anything you please! Now, let me see you disobey that!"

The dirty little boy came in from playing out-of-doors and asked his mother, "Who am I?"

Guessing, the mother replied, "Tarzan?"

The boy replied, "Then the lady down the street was right."

"About what?" questioned his mother.

"She said I was so dirty my own mother wouldn't recognize me!"

David: "Mother, may I be a preacher when I grow up?"

Mother: "I suppose you can. But are you sure that's what you want to be?"

David: "Well, I've got to go to church anyhow, and since I hate to sit still and be quiet, I'd rather go to church and stand up and holler."

A man who usually took a bus to work overslept one morning and decided to drive. As he opened the garage door he saw that the rear wall—the one his wife smashed when she stepped on the gas pedal instead of the brake—had not been repaired. He strode back into the house and telephoned the carpenter. "You said that you would have it fixed by noon yesterday," he stormed.

"Let me ask you one question," said the carpenter quietly. "Did your wife drive the car in the afternoon?"

"I want you to know in advance," the surgeon told his patient, "that I'm in favor of getting my patients up and around very quickly. Three hours after surgery you will sit up, five hours later you will stand up, and the next morning you will walk around on the nurse's arm. That afternoon you will start to walk again unaided."

"All right," replied the patient. "I guess you know what you are doing, but I have a request to make."

"Certainly, Sir," said the surgeon. "What is it?"

"Would it be OK," asked the patient, "if I lie down a little while during the operation?"

One night I spent all night out on the lawn trying to kill the garden hose.

Sergeant: "I suppose after you get out of the army you'll be waiting for me to die, just so you can go to my funeral and laugh."

Rookie: "No, Sarge. After I shed this uniform I don't want to ever stand in line again!"

The minister was having Sunday dinner with the Fosters and asked little Jonathan, "You don't go fishing on Sunday do you, Jonathan?"

"No. No, Sir. Never."

"That's very good, but can you tell me why?"

"Oh, yes Sir. My daddy says he doesn't want to be bothered with me!"

Golf is a sport that controls your nerves, toughens your muscles, improves your health and increases your stamina so you are strong enough to play again next week.

It's astonishing how long it takes to finish something you are not working on.

If you consult enough experts you can confirm any opinion.

Perfection

Bragged the husband, "My wife is just as beautiful today as she was the day I married her." He paused and added, "Of course, it does take her longer."

A neighbor came down the sidewalk, desperately following the big dog on a leash.

"Well, Jim," said Joe, pausing with his rake and basket, "haven't seen you along here in the evenings this fall. Where have you been keeping yourself?"

Jim gave a mighty yank on the leash and yelled, "Whoa, Prince! Well," he said, "I've been taking Prince to obedience school."

"Is that so?" Joe remarked, looking skeptically at the big animal. "And how's it going? Has he learned to obey?"

"Does everything I say," replied Jim. "Watch this: Prince! Lunge on your leash, boy. Good boy! Whine and bark, boy. Good boy! Run around in an agitated manner and tangle the leash around my ankles, Prince. Good boy! There, how about that? He not only does everything I tell him, but does them all at once. One well-trained dog, wouldn't you say?"

"Yep," Joe observed, rubbing his hand down over his chin. "And smart, too. He even anticipates your commands."

Don't worry about computers taking over our lives. If they get too powerful, we can just organize them into committees.

Ed: "Can you name five days in a week without naming Monday, Tuesday, Wednesday, Thursday, or Friday?"
John: "No, of course not! Can you?"
Ed: "Certainly! Today, day before yesterday, yesterday, tomorrow, and the next day!"

A long-winded speaker was interrupted by a voice from the rear yelling, "Louder." After the third time a fellow in the front row stood up, faced the rear of the room and asked, "Can't you hear?"
"No."
"Then thank God and keep still."

Finally the long-staying guest was ready to leave. "Goodnight," he said. "I hope I haven't kept you up too late."
The yawning host replied, "Not at all. We need to be getting up soon anyway."

A local hero's deed of valor was immortalized in a life-sized painting, done by a hometown artist who was not exactly a professional. When the great night of the unveiling came, the subject viewed the portrait and finally said to the committee, "Gentlemen—it's a beautiful frame!"

Esther: "I'm always breaking into song."
Pam: "You wouldn't need to if you had the key."

My statistics are 100 percent accurate 5 percent of the time.

Uncle Zeke was never caught without words. As he walked by the blacksmith shop, the blacksmith had inadvertently flipped a hot horseshoe over into the sand in his path. Uncle Zeke picked up the horseshoe, discovered it was hot, and flipped it away instantly.

Several kids who observed the incident thought they had found Uncle Zeke in his first predicament without words.

"What's the matter, Uncle Zeke, was the horseshoe hot?"

"No," said Uncle Zeke calmly, "it just don't take me long to look at a horseshoe."

A clergyman had preached on the subject of Jacob's ladder, and his young son was very impressed. A few days later he told his father that he had dreamed about the discourse.

"And what did you see, my son?"

"I dreamed," replied the boy, "that I saw a ladder reaching up into the clouds. At the foot of the ladder were many pieces of chalk, and no one was allowed to climb up without taking a piece of chalk and marking on each rung for each sin committed."

"Very interesting, my boy, and what else?"

"Well, Father, I thought I would go up, but I hadn't gotten very far when I heard someone coming down."

"Yes," said the father, "and who was that?"

"You, Father," replied the boy.

"Me? Whatever was I coming down for?"

"More chalk!" came the reply.

"Miss Wilcox," a chap told his new secretary firmly, "always add a column of figures at least three times before you show me the result."

The next day she came in with a broad smile, "Mr. Johnson," she said, "I added those figures ten times."

"Good, I like a girl to be thorough."

"And here," she said, "are my ten answers."

A housewife called up a pet store and said, "Send me thirty thousand cockroaches at once."

"What in the world do you want with thirty thousand cockroaches?" asked the astonished salesclerk.

"Well," replied the woman, "I am moving today, and my lease says I must leave the premises here in exactly the same condition I found them."

PERFECTION—a lady who finds what she wants on the first dive into her handbag.

Wife: "Doctor, I want you to tell me the truth. Is there any hope for my husband?"

Doctor: "Ma'am, I'm afraid he can't recover, but to make sure, I'm going to call in another doctor."

"I want to exchange these snakeskin shoes," the woman told the clerk in the crowded shoe store. "See those scratches—the shoes are imperfect!"

The clerk noted the tiny scratches and brought out another pair. The lady examined them carefully and commented, "These are marred, too."

A few minutes later the clerk returned with six pairs of shoes. The customer found a flaw in each pair. "They are all imperfect!" she exclaimed as she discarded the last one.

"Madam," said the salesman wearily, "I'm not perfect; you're not perfect. How can you expect a snake to be perfect?"

Poverty

Most people don't care how much they pay for something, as long as it isn't all at once!

During his early days in New York, a humorist-illustrator could not pay his hotel bill. The manager did not press him for the money, but at the end of each week he would send him a new bill for a larger amount.

One morning when the two met in the lobby the manager asked, "Did you get the latest bill?"

"Yes," said the artist.

"Is that all you have to say?"

"At the moment, yes, but if the bill gets any larger, I will have to ask you for a larger room."

A beggar appeared at the door of a boy's dormitory. A student opened the door and heard the unfortunate one's plea.

"Has Fortune never knocked on your door?" asked the student.

"He did once," replied the beggar, "but I was out. Ever since, he has sent his daughter."

"His daughter!" exclaimed the puzzled student. "Who is she?"

"Why, can it be possible that you do not know Fortune's daughter? It's Miss Fortune, of course."

We fought the war on poverty long before it was invented, and we lost. Actually, we were prisoners of war.

Did you hear about the Texan who just bought his son a cowboy outfit—a twenty-thousand acre ranch, one thousand head of cattle, and two hundred horses?

"I lost a fortune!"

"How?"

"Well, yesterday I felt like a million, and now I feel like two cents!"

It's beginning to look as if those who maintain that the world owes them a living are going to win.

A panhandler, dirty, shabbily dressed, and unshaven, approached a well-dressed gentleman on the street and said, "I am a totally worthless individual, unmotivated by any desire for self-betterment, devoid of even a vestige of pride or human dignity. I am a millstone around the neck of society, and, in summation, a discredit to the American way of life and the human race. That will be five dollars please."

Minister's wife: "Wake up! There are burglars in our house!"
Minister: "So—what of it? Let them find out their mistake by themselves."

A man's relatives were gathered for the reading of his will after his death.

"This is going to be brief," said the lawyer. "I read as follows:

"'Being of sound mind, I spent every last cent before I died.'"

"Boss, I have to have a raise," the man said to his boss. "There are three other companies after me."

"Is that so?" asked the manager. "What other companies are after you?"

"The electric company, the telephone company, and the gas company."

A traveler stopped at a historic old hotel and asked the clerk for the nightly rate for a single room.

"A room on the first floor is fifty dollars; on the second floor, forty dollars; and on the third thirty dollars," answered the clerk.

The man looked around and then turned to go.

"Don't you find the hotel attractive?" asked the clerk.

"Oh, it's beautiful—it just isn't tall enough!"

Father (to son at college graduation): "I know you want to be a salesman, but take it from me, go into poverty. That's where all the money is."

Procrastination

A worried-looking gentleman hurried into a florist shop and asked for potted chrysanthemums.

"I'm sorry, Sir," replied the clerk, "we're out of chrysanthemums. How about geraniums?"

"No, that won't do," answered the gentleman. "I promised my wife I would water her chrysanthemums while she was gone."

Tom: "Have you ever been married?"

Russ: "Yes, but my wife left me."

Tom: "How did that happen?"

Russ: "She ran away while I was taking a bath."

Tom: "I'll bet she waited years for the chance."

The garageman answered the distress call of a man whose car had stalled. A quick check showed he had run out of gas and he told him so.

"Will it hurt," he asked, "if I drive it home with the gasoline tank empty? I'm in quite a hurry."

A bum stopped a man on the street and asked for a handout. "I'm sorry, but I don't have any change," said the man. "But I tell you what I'll do. I'm on my way to the bank, and on my way back I'll give you something."

"Afraid that won't do," answered the beggar. "You'd be surprised how much I've lost giving credit that way."

Smith: "Hello, I just thought I'd drop in and get the umbrella you borrowed from me last week."

Jones: "I'm awfully sorry. I lent it to a friend. Do you need it?"

Smith: "Well, not for myself. But the fellow I borrowed it from says the owner wants it back."

"Wouldn't it be neat to know the time and place that you were to die?" asked a frivolous teenage girl.

"What good would that be?" asked her boyfriend.

"I wouldn't show up," she said.

After a hard game of racquetball one man said to his friend, "Well, shall we play again next Saturday?"

The friend replied, "I was going to get married on Sunday, but I can put it off."

The young preacher was asked what was meant by procrastination. "I don't really know," he replied, "but it's something the Presbyterians believe in."

After a late night staff meeting at the office, a man went "out on the town" with several other men. He was having such a good time that it was morning before he knew it, and he decided he should call his wife with some sort of explanation.

When his wife answered the phone he put all the excitement he could into his voice and said, "Honey, don't pay the ransom. I've escaped."

Husband: "Why do you want me to walk you to the garbage can?"

Wife: "So that I can tell my friends we go out together once in awhile."

He's a man of firm convictions. This manifests itself as soon as he knows what anyone else thinks on a given subject.

Reducing

The hardest kind of diet pill to take is the one who keeps telling you how to do it.

If one is really serious about losing weight, one must give up only three things: breakfast, lunch, and dinner.

Marge: "I've lost fifteen pounds!"
Ruth: "Well, turn around—I think I've found them."

My husband is on a strict diet—bananas and coconuts. He's not losing any weight, but you should see him climb a tree.

Eat, drink and be merry—for tomorrow you diet.

Did you hear about the latest dieting craze—garlic sandwiches. You don't lose any weight but from afar you look smaller.

The best way to reduce your weight is to eat all you want of everything you don't want.

Dieting is recommended only for those who are thick and tired of it.

Diet: What helps a person gain weight more slowly.

You can't reduce by talking about reducing. It's better to keep your mouth shut.

A heavyset man asked his petite wife, "Have you seen my belt around the house?"
"Is it around the house?" she asked.

Weight loss is wishful shrinking.

An overweight teenager was discussing his tennis game: "When an opponent hits a ball to me, my brain immediately commands my body to do the following: 'Race up to the blistering drive and slice it to the far corner of the court, jump back into position to return the next volley'; then my body says, 'Who, me?'"

The waist is a terrible thing to mind.

A gaunt, hungry-looking panhandler edged up to a plump, well-dressed matron.
"Madam," he said, "I haven't eaten for four days."
"For goodness sakes," she said admiringly, "I wish I had your willpower."

A guest said to a little boy, "Sonny, what will you do when you are as big as your father?"
Replied the honest little boy, "Diet."

A heavyset man arrived at a small country town. He happened to see an old-time penny scale outside the store with an engraved sign which read: "Your weight for a penny." *What a break,* he thought. He stepped on the scale and dropped in a penny. After a short pause a polite female voice came through the speaker on the scale, "Deposit twenty-four more cents, please."

Mr. Barnes was reading his evening paper. Mrs. Barnes was working on a dress she was making for herself. Said Mr. Barnes, "Honey, here's a tent and awning sale in case you run out of material for your dress!"

Before they were married, his chin was his best feature—now it's a double feature.

I'm not going to starve to death just so I can live a little longer.

Restaurants

A man visiting a strange town walked into a small cafe. When the waitress came to take his order, the man said, "Chicken casserole and a kind word."

A few minutes later the waitress returned and set his meal before him. The man replied, "Where's the kind word?"

The waitress sighed and whispered, "Don't eat the chicken casserole."

Irritated customer: "Do you serve crabs in this rat hole?"
Waiter: "Yes, sir. What can I get you?"

Customer: "Your ad says you will pay seventy-five dollars to anyone who orders something you can't serve. I would like to order an elephant ear sandwich."

Waitress: "Oh, no! I guess we owe you seventy-five dollars."

Customer: "You don't have elephant ears, then?"

Waitress: "Yes, we've got plenty of elephant ears, but we're all out of the big buns."

Craig: "I hate to talk about the cook, but you'll notice three shakers on each table, salt, pepper, and Alka Seltzer."

Waitress: "How is the soup today, ma'am?"

Diner: "Well, to be honest, I'm sorry I stirred it."

Customer to waiter: "Why is this steak so small? Last night I had one twice this size."

Waiter: "Where were you sitting?"

Customer: "Over by the window. But what does that matter?"

Waiter: "That's simple. We always serve large portions by the window. It's good advertising."

My wife is such a great cook she has to call in the repairman to fix a TV dinner. She constantly serves leftovers. It's like eating reruns.

"Jack, why did the gentleman sitting at table three leave so quickly?" asked the restaurant manager of the waiter.

"I'm not really sure," replied the waiter. "He asked for sausages, and I told him we were all out of them, but if he could wait for a few minutes, I'd get the cook to make some. I went to the kitchen, and as I set down a tray of dishes, I stepped on the dog's tail and he let out a wild yelp. Then when I came back into the dining room, the man was on his way out the door!"

Customer: "I don't like the looks of that haddock."

Waitress: "Lady, if it's looks you're after, why don't you buy a goldfish?"

Customer: "How long do I have to wait for the half portion of duck I ordered?"

Waiter: "Until someone orders the other half—we just can't go out and kill half a duck."

When a busload of people entered a large restaurant, the leader of the group approached the manager.

"Sir, I'm Mr. Underwood of the Halfway House. These nice folks are former mental patients. They've all been cured, but they do have one small problem: they will want to pay you in bottle caps. So, if you'll be so kind as to humor them in this way, I'll take care of the bill when they are through."

The manager, wanting to be a good citizen, went along and collected the bottle caps. The leader returned and with gratitude said, "Thanks so much. I'll pay the bill now. Do you have change for a hubcap?"

Salesmen

A salesman told her he had a vacuum cleaner that would cut her housework in half. So she bought two of them.

A salesman was on a business trip and was snowed in by a blizzard. He sent a telegram to his office that said: "Snowbound. Will not be able to leave my hotel for one week. Stop. Can't sell anything here. Stop. What shall I do now?"

The sales manager wired back: "Start your vacation immediately."

115

A shy salesman visited the doctor and was advised he needed to toughen himself up. The doctor suggested he start at home, rather than out in public.

That evening the usually quiet man said to his wife, "I will be giving the orders from now on. After you serve my dinner, I want you to lay out my best clothes; I will be going out alone this evening. And do you know who's going to dress me in my tuxedo and black tie?"

"I certainly do," declared his wife, "the undertaker!"

Sales manager to salesman: "I'm going to give you a raise—I want your last week to be a happy one!"

"Sir, may I please have Thursday off?" a timid employee asked his boss. "My wife and I will be celebrating our silver anniversary."

Retorted the boss, "Am I going to have to put up with this every twenty-five years?"

A salesman was stating his qualifications for a new job. "I have been very successful in every sales job I have ever had. I don't mind long hours, I can sell anything to anybody, and I really enjoy my work," he stated to the sales manager.

"Do you smoke?" asked the sales manager.

"No, Sir."

"Do you drink?"

"Never touch the stuff."

"Do you chase other women?"

"Oh, no, Sir. I'm a very happily married man with four children."

Highly impressed by the man, the sales manager finally asked, "Don't you have any bad habits?"

Confessed the salesman, "Well, yes. Just one. I'm the world's biggest liar."

A sales manager was giving his new salesman a minute-by-minute schedule for his first sales trip.

"Here is your schedule," said the manager. "Now be sure to follow it to the minute."

It read: 7:15 AM—arrive at airport; 7:30 AM—take Eastern flight 742; 8:45 AM—arrive at Chicago airport and have a cup of coffee; 9:12 AM—take a cab to client's office.

A little after 9:00 AM the sales manager received a telegram from the new salesman. It read, "No cream for coffee in cafe. What do I do now?"

At a sales convention a salesman received a telegram which he opened and immediately threw in a wastebasket.

Asked a friend, "Who was the telegram from?"

"My wife."

The friend took the letter from the wastebasket and looked at it. "Why, there's nothing written on it. It's just a blank piece of paper."

"I know," answered the salesman. "My wife got mad at me when I wouldn't let her come to the convention. Now, she's not speaking to me."

Retired salesman to elderly girlfriend: "I seem to be getting a little forgetful. Did I ask you to marry me last night?"

Elderly girlfriend: "Well, someone did, but I've forgotten who it was!"

A successful salesman was arguing with one of his competitors and said, "There are plenty of ways to make money, but there is only one honest way."

"And what way is that?" asked his competitor.

Retorted the first man, "I should've known you wouldn't know!"

Once upon a time a tiger ate a bull. He felt so good that he growled and growled. A hunter heard him growling and killed him with just one shot.

Moral: When you are full of bull, keep your mouth shut.

A salesman asked his secretary, "Who was that on the telephone?"

"I don't know," she answered. "She just said, 'Long distance from Chicago,' so I said, 'yes, it sure is,' and hung up."

A salesman rang the doorbell and smiled when a middle-aged woman appeared.

"May I speak to the lady of the house?"

"Yes, unless you are blind!" the woman answered belligerently.

"Please excuse me, ma'am! Are you the lady of the house?"

"Of course I am. Who did you take me for? The gentleman of the house, the next-door neighbor, the cat, or the butler?"

"I wasn't sure, ma'am. I thought you might be the youngest daughter."

She replied with a smile, "Oh? And what can I do for you?"

A shoe salesman had dragged out half of his stock to show a lady customer. Finally, he said, "Excuse me, lady, do you mind if I take a break? Your feet are killing me."

A man selling children's encyclopedias was concluding a high-pressure sales pitch. As the housewife hesitated, he turned to her young son and said, "Little boy, ask me any question—anything you want to know. I will show you and your mother where you can find the answer in this wonderful book."

"OK," said the little boy, "what kind of car does God drive?"

A salesman went into a small grocery store to buy a box of soda. The shelves of the entire store were filled with thousands of jars of mayonnaise. In order to get the soda the owner of the store had to go to the basement. The salesman went with him and couldn't believe it when he found the basement was stacked with cartons of mayonnaise on all sides.

"Hey," said the salesman, "you must sell a lot of mayonnaise."

Answered the grocer, "No, I can't sell mayonnaise at all. But that fellow who sells me mayonnaise! Boy! Can he sell mayonnaise!"

Chicken to pig: "Hey, let's open a restaurant featuring ham and eggs. We could make a fortune."

Pig: "It's easy for you to get enthused about this. For you it's just a contribution; for me it's a total commitment!"

The sales manager of a large corporation was horrified when he discovered their newest salesman, Johnson, was actually illiterate. He was just about to fire him when he received a note from Johnson. It read:

"Dat Chicago compiny dat ain't ever bot frum us. Wel, I sole dem $150,000. Now I go to Spreengfel."

The next day the sales manager received another note from Johnson.

"Dat compiny in Spreengfel dat ain't ever bot nothin'. I sole dem haf a million."

The sales manager posted the notes on the bulletin board along with a note with these words:

"We ben spendin' to much time tryin' to spil insted of tryin' to sel. Johnson, who is out on the rode, is doin' a grate job for us. You shuld go out an do like he dun."

Because of a computer error, the salesman's paycheck envelope contained a blank check. "Look," he said, showing the check to his wife, "this is what I've been afraid of! My deductions have finally caught up with my salary."

119

A man walked in a men's clothing store and told the sales manager he wanted a job as a salesman.

"Sorry, we don't need any salesmen," the manager told him.

"But, you've just got to hire me," the man said. "I'm not just your ordinary salesman. I'm the world's greatest salesman!"

The sales manager again refused, but the man hung on and was so convincing that finally the manager said, "OK, I'll tell you what I'll do. See that suit over there hanging on the back wall. After you've dusted it off, you'll see that it has padded shoulders, pointed lapels, and a belt in the back. It's sort of a blue-orange-green-purple plaid. I don't even remember how I got stuck with it. Now, I'm going to lunch and I'm going to leave you in charge. If you can sell that suit before I get back, you're hired."

About an hour later the sales manager returned to find the store was a mess. The rugs were ripped, a showcase was turned over, and merchandise was all over the floor. But the suit was gone.

"Well, I see you've sold the suit."

"Yes, Sir."

"It looks like you had a little trouble with the customer, though."

"No, Sir. Not a bit of trouble with the customer, but oh, that seeing-eye dog."

His manager has received offers from several publishers for the fiction rights to his expense accounts.

School

Joe: "I understand your son is in college. Is he going to be a lawyer, doctor, or engineer, perhaps?"

Ted: "I'm not really sure. The question right now is will he become a sophomore?"

Bart: "Did you pass your exams?"
Rick: "Did I!"
Bart: "Were they easy?"
Rick: "I don't know; ask Fred."

A college student wrote home to his parents: "Dear Mom and Dad: I haven't heard from you in a long time. Please send a check so I'll know that you are all right."

A scientist was doing research on centipedes. Each day he would cut several legs off the centipede and demand that the centipede hobble over to his food and "eat!"

Finally, when the centipede was down to two legs, the scientist demanded that he "eat!" The centipede, of course, didn't move.

The scientist wrote in his book, "Cutting off the legs of centipedes causes them to become hard of hearing and to lose their appetite."

Ben: "Why do the janitors here at school wear uniforms?"
Tom: "So we can tell them from the faculty."

Professor (frowning angrily): "Sir, whatever made you write a paragraph like that?"
Student: "Well, I thought it would be all right to quote Dickens."
Professor: "A beautiful passage, isn't it?"

The schoolteacher was horrified when she saw the picture one of her pupils had drawn. "Why it looks like a cowboy walking into a saloon," she said.

"It is," said the child. "But it's all right. He's not going to drink anything; he's just going in to shoot a man."

The little boy went into the grocery store and reading from a book told the grocer, "Put down ten pounds of sugar at twenty cents a pound, four pounds of coffee at eighty cents a pound, two pounds of butter at seventy-two cents a pound, and two bars of soap at fifteen cents each."

"OK, I've got that down," said the grocer.

"How much does that come to?" asked the boy.

"Six dollars and ninety-four cents."

"Well, if I gave you a ten dollar bill how much change would I get?" said the boy.

"Three dollars and six cents," said the impatient grocer. "Come on, I'm in a hurry."

"Oh, I don't want to buy them," said the boy as he disappeared through the door; "that's our arithmetic lesson for tomorrow, and I needed some help with it."

Teacher: "If there were four flies on the table and I killed one, how many would be left?"

Student: "One. The dead one."

A young girl was taking a civil service examination. One of the questions was: "If a man buys an article for $13.25 and sells it for $8.75, does he gain or lose by the transaction?"

The young girl thought for a long time and answered, "He gains on the cents but loses on the dollars."

College freshman: "Hey, Dad, you are a lucky man."

Father: "Why is that?"

Freshman: "You won't have to buy new books for me this year. I'm taking last year's work again."

Father: "How can you say that dating while in college keeps you young?"

Son: "Well, I started dating two years ago as a sophomore, and I'm still a sophomore."

Professor: "What three words are most used among college students?"
Student: "I don't know."
Professor: "Exactly."

To steal ideas from one person is plagiarism; to steal ideas from many is research.

Dear Dad,
You haven't sent me a check in several weeks. What kind of kindness is that?
Love, your son

Dear Son,
This is known as "unremitting kindness."
Love, Dad

Secretaries

The office manager of a large corporation went over to the desk of a pretty young secretary and asked, "Miss Brown, are you doing anything Sunday night?"
"Well, no," answered the girl.
"Then get a good night's sleep and try to get to work on time Monday."

Executive: "Where is my pencil?"
Secretary: "Behind your ear."
Executive: "Come, come girl. I'm a busy man. Which ear?"

New typist (following rapid-fire dictation): "Now, Mr. Jones, what did you say between 'Dear Sir' and 'Sincerely yours?'"

A memorandum on a phone call was handed to a businessman by his secretary.

"I can't read this," he said.

"I couldn't understand him very well," said the secretary. "So I didn't write it very clearly."

The boss was exasperated with his new secretary. She ignored the telephone when it rang. Finally he said, irritably, "You must answer the telephone."

The secretary replied, "OK, but it seems so silly. Nine out of ten it's for you."

The president called his office manager in and threw a letter full of errors before him.

"Look at that! I thought I told you to engage a new stenographer on the basis of her grammar!"

The office manager looked startled, "Grammar? I thought you said glamour."

The secretary kept turning pages of the dictionary until finally another office worker asked what she was trying to find.

"Bankruptcy," said the first girl.

"Well, why are you looking way back there?"

"I know how to spell bank," she replied, "and now I'm looking for ruptcy."

"Did you ask the boss for a raise?" the stenographer asked the girl at the next desk who had just returned from the inner office.

"Yes, and he was a perfect lamb, just as I had expected."

"Oh, what did he say?"

"Bah!"

Boss: "Well, did you read the letter I sent you?"

Secretary: "Oh, yes, Sir. It said, 'You're fired' on the inside; but on the outside it said, 'Return in five days,' so here I am!"

The doctor's new secretary was puzzled by an entry in the doctor's notes on an emergency case: "Shot in the lumbar region," it read. After a moment she typed in the record, "Shot in the woods."

Never walk down a hallway of an office building without a piece of paper in your hand.

Never fails—when something is confidential it is left in the copying machine.

It's complicated to soar with eagles when you work with turkeys.

Shopping

Wife to husband: "I cut down on our expenses last month. I charged everything on one credit card so that it will only take one postage stamp to pay the bill."

Customer: "What! Six hundred dollars for that antique desk? Just last week I priced it, and you said five hundred and twenty-five dollars."

Businessman: "I know, but the cost of materials and labor has gone up so much!"

A man finally bought a parrot at an auction after some very vivacious bidding.

"I suppose this bird does talk," he said to the auctioneer.

"Does he talk? Why, he's been bidding against you for the past twenty minutes!"

One day a large department store had a sale on ladies' hosiery. A dignified, middle-aged gentleman decided to get his wife a pair. Soon he found himself being pushed and shoved by frantic women. He took as much as he could. Then he plowed through the crowd, trying to make his way to the aisle.

"Hey, you," demanded a frustrated shopper, "can't you act like a gentleman?"

"What do you mean?" the gentleman replied. "I've been acting like a gentleman for half an hour. From now on, I'm going to act like a lady!"

A wise wife asks her husband for something she knows he can't afford, so she can compromise on what she really wants.

An architect was having a difficult time with a prospective home builder. "Can't you at least give me *some* idea of the type of house you want to build?" pleaded the architect.

The man hesitated, then replied, "Well, all I can tell you is it must go with an antique doorknob my wife bought in Boston."

Looking for an inexpensive gift for a friend, a penny pincher went into a gift shop but found everything too expensive.

He priced a glass vase that had been broken and found that he could buy it for almost nothing. He asked the store to send it, hoping his friend would think it had been broken in the mail.

After a while he received a note from his friend that read:

"Thank you for the vase. It was so thoughtful of you to wrap each piece separately."

Sickness

Medical statistics show that one of every four persons are mentally ill. Next time you are one of a group of four, take a good look at the other three. If they are not, you're it.

Man to psychiatrist: "Doctor, every once in a while I get this very strong feeling that I'm a dog."
Psychiatrist: "Well, let's talk about it. Come, lie on the couch."
Sick man: "Oh, I'm not allowed on the couch."

A woman walked into a psychiatrist's office with a strip of bacon over each ear and a fried egg on top of her head and said, "I've come to talk to you about my brother."

A doctor was taken to a patient's room but came down after a few minutes and asked for a screwdriver. Several minutes later he asked for a can opener. Shortly thereafter, he returned and asked for a hammer and a saw. The worried wife couldn't stand it any longer and asked, "Doctor, please tell me. What's wrong with my husband?"

"I don't know yet," answered the frustrated doctor, "I can't get my bag open."

My wife was very ill, so we called Dr. Thomas. My wife took her medicine and got worse. So we called Dr. Hill. She took her medicine and still got worse. We were afraid she was going to die, so we called Dr. Anderson. He was too busy. Finally, my wife got well.

Socialized medicine is when grownups get together and talk about their operations.

Doctor: "I'm sorry to have to tell you, but your husband's mind is completely gone."
Wife: "Well, I'm not surprised. He has been giving me a piece of it for eighteen years."

The impatient old man got tired of sitting in the waiting room to see the doctor. Finally, he told the nurse, "I guess I'll just go home and die a natural death."

She's always collecting ills and pills and getting chills.

He's one of the chronic invalids who have every ailment and disease described on television.

When nothing makes her sick, that's exactly what makes her sick.

When she has a sore throat she doesn't go to a doctor. She sits in front of her television with her mouth open so the actor playing the doctor's part can see her tonsils.

Nurse: "How are *we* today? Are *we* taking *our* pills? You know what happens if *we* don't?"
Patient: "Yes, *we* will die and *they* will bury *us*!"

The medical community was thrilled to learn that today researchers found a cure for which there is no known disease.

After three days in the hospital, I took a turn for the nurse.

Arthur: "My friend was operated on for kidney trouble, and four days later he died of heart trouble."

Don: "My doctor is a specialist. If he operates for kidney trouble, you die of kidney trouble, and it doesn't take four days either!"

Roy: "I've mastered meditation. I'm just humming along. I feel completely balanced, centered, aligned, and energized."

Dan: "Is this from meditation or did you get yourself a lube job?"

My dad believed in meditation. He used to tell me, "Sit down and shut up!"

Singles

Phyllis: "What is the most important to you when looking for a husband—wealth, appearance, or brains?"

Donna: "Appearance—and the sooner the better."

Brad: "Why aren't you married?"

John: "I was born this way."

Cindy: "Does Bruce ever intend to get married?"

Tammy: "I don't think so. He's studying for his bachelor's degree."

Young girl to friend: "That Tom has not only ruined my life, shattered my hopes and dreams, but he's also wrecked my whole evening!"

Wedding reception guest: "Young man, are you the bridegroom?"

Young man: "No, Ma'am. I lost out in the semifinals."

A single Texan who was brooding over the fact that he was living in the second largest state went to Alaska and asked, "How do I get to be an Alaskan?"

A citizen, figuring on having a little fun with him, said, "Podnah, you can't be full-blooded Alaskan until you've downed a pint of whiskey in one gulp, kissed a single Eskimo girl, and shot a polar bear."

"That's for me," said the Texan and ordered the pint of whiskey. He got it down in one gulp, although his eyes were glazing slightly as he lurched from the saloon. The boys waited for him until almost midnight when he stumbled through the door all scratched and ripped and bloody.

"OK," he said, "I'm gonna be an Alaskan. Now where's that single Eskimo girl I'm supposed to shoot?"

A sophisticated young single lady was asked to attend a public function. She was assigned a place between a noted bishop and an equally famous rabbi.

"I feel as if I were the page between the Old and New Testaments," she said brilliantly, during a lull in the conversation.

"That page, madam," replied the rabbi, "is usually blank."

Maggie: "If you could have two wishes, what would they be?"

Marianne: "Well, I think I'd wish for a husband."

Maggie: "That's only one wish. What is your other one?"

Marianne: "I would have to save the other until I saw how he turned out."

An old man was talking to a young bachelor and asked him why he hadn't married. The bachelor proceeded to tell him about different women he had dated, finding fault with each. But it appeared that each of the women had succeeded in getting married.

"You are in danger of getting left out," said the old man. "You better hurry before it's too late."

"Oh," said the bachelor, "there are plenty of good fish left in the sea."

"Yes, that may be true," pointed out the kind, old man. "But what about the bait? Isn't there the danger it might get stale?"

Joan: "Is Ken a confirmed bachelor?"
Lynn: "He sure is. He sent his picture to a lonely hearts club and they returned it saying, 'We're not that lonely!'"

Miss Miller: "I know that he is rich, but isn't he a little too old to be considered eligible?"
Miss Wallace: "Certainly not. He's too eligible to be considered old."

A police chief received a letter from a woman in another city who asked him to find the perfect man so she could marry him. Here were her specifications: a man about fifty with no children, preferably a doctor or banker or lawyer. The police chief sent the letter to the Bureau of Missing Persons.

A bashful young man, with a good deal of assistance from his girlfriend, finally proposed and was promptly accepted. There followed a long silence. At last the girl said, "Well, now that we are engaged, why don't you say something about it?"

The young man replied, "I think there's been too much said about it already."

Two men were talking about marriage. One said he had married a widow. "I couldn't stand being a widow's second husband," said the man who wasn't married. Said the other, "I'd rather be a widow's second husband than her first."

Sports

A foreigner stopped for lunch in a small town and noticing he was opposite a college, decided to take a look at the place. As he passed a student on the campus, he stopped the lad and asked the name of the college.

"Sorry, Sir, I really don't know," he muttered. "I'm just a football player here."

Sign on fence bordering golf course: "Attention Golfers. We are raising small children behind this fence, so please refrain from enriching their vocabularies. Thank you!"

"It's not that I really cheat," the golfer explained, "it's just that I play for my health, and a low score makes me feel better."

Then there was the fellow who went to the tennis match in a starched collar and sawed his head off.

The little church in the suburbs suddenly stopped buying from its regular office supply dealer, and so he telephoned a deacon to ask why.

"I'll tell you why," replied the deacon with some indignation. "We ordered some pencils from you, to be used in the pews for visitors to register."

"Well," interrupted the dealer, "didn't you receive them yet?"

"Oh, we received some pencils all right," replied the deacon. "But you sent us some golf pencils, each stamped with the words, 'Play Golf Next Sunday.'"

"OK, men," said the football coach at the end of a discouraging practice session, "There's one more formation I want to teach you. It's pretty simple—everybody just form a circle around me."

The players gathered around him. "Now start running toward the field house," he ordered.

"But coach," exclaimed one player, "when will we need a formation like this?"

"If things go as I suspect," replied the coach, "it'll be needed for every game—to get me past the alumni."

When a baseball scout signed up a teenage pitcher, the front office wired the lad to report immediately to the farm club. The following day the secretary received a collect call from the rookie. "Gee, Mr. Morton, do you mind if I don't report for another couple of days?" he pleaded.

Surprised, the official asked why.

"I haven't had time to make the collections on my paper route yet," the boy replied.

Several years ago, a big league umpire was hired in the off-season by a Hollywood movie company to operate behind the plate during the filming of a sports picture. As the scene opened, the pitcher wound up and delivered the ball. The umpire yelled, "Ball."

"Cut," shouted the director angrily, "you're not following the script. That pitch was supposed to be a strike."

"Don't tell me to follow the script," roared the umpire, "tell the pitcher to follow it. I call 'em as I see 'em."

A stomach specialist from a big city has a formula for patients with nervous indigestion. He asks them if they play golf. If they say yes, he tells them to cut it out. If they say no, he tells them to start playing.

A proud father was approached by his neighbor, "I heard your son graduated from college. Congratulations!"

The neighbor hesitated and said, "Isn't it awfully expensive to send a boy to college nowadays?"

Said the father, "It sure is. It cost me thousands of dollars, and all I got was a quarterback."

A small boy had fallen into a stream but had been rescued. "How did you come to fall in?" asked a bystander.

"I didn't come to fall in," explained the boy, "I came to fish and slipped off that log."

I see what's wrong, thought the umpire, as threats and nasty remarks were coming from every direction for his last decision. *The umpire should be stationed in the grandstand.*

Coach (to new player): "You're fantastic! The way you hammer the line, dodge, tackle, and worm through your opponents is great."

Modest player: "I guess it all comes from early training, sir. See, my mom used to take me shopping with her on sale days."

Golf was based on an old Roman game of paganicus, which was played with a bent stick and a leather ball filled with feathers. The name was changed to golf because most of the professionals refused to join a club called the Professional Paganicus Association.

In 1457 King James II banned "golfe" (as well as "futeball") because the popularity of the game threatened the practice of archery as a national defense. Even today, husbands still suffer the slings and arrows of their wives who just don't quite understand.

"Caddy, why you keep looking at your watch?"
"Sorry, Sir, it's not a watch—it's a compass."

"Excuse me—please let me play through."
"What's your hurry?"
"The battery on my golf cart is running down."

"I gave up fishing to take up golf. And I like golf much better."
"How come?"
"Because when you lie about golf, you don't have to show anybody anything."

New golfer: "I want to be a golfer in the worst way."
Caddy: "Well, it looks as if you've already made it."

"I'm sorry sir, but we don't have any open time on the course today."
"Yeah? What if Jack Nicklaus and Tom Weiskopf showed up? I'll bet you would find a tee time for them."
"Of course we would."
"Well, I just happen to know they are not coming, so I'll take their time."

Mike: "You've been a baseball player, a football player, a skier, a surfer, a track star, a hockey player; have you been anything else?"
Will: "Yes, exhausted."

Riley: "As a track star, weren't you an expert with the javelin?"

Lonnie: "I'm one of the few to ever throw a javelin two hundred yards."

Riley: "That's amazing—two hundred yards."

Lonnie: "Well, I actually threw it only one hundred yards. The guy it hit crawled the other hundred."

Lloyd: "Where do you raise your bulls?"

Keith: "I raise them on my own ranch and bring them into the ring in a little cart which I made myself. I call it a Bull Buggy."

"It's kind of surprising to see an empty seat for this football game. It's the hottest ticket in town."

"I can explain that. See, my wife and I bought tickets for this game several months ago, and since then she died."

"Oh, that's too bad. Couldn't you bring a friend?"

"No, they are all at the funeral."

Teenagers

Father of teenage son: "My son has developed a case of cauliflower ear—not from boxing—but from talking on the telephone."

Teenage daughter to father: "Dad, my allowance has fallen below the national average for teenagers."

Teenage son: "Dad, if you don't let me use the car tonight according to the Bible you hate me."

Father: "Just where does it say that?"

Teenage son: "'He that spareth his "rod" hateth his son,' Proverbs 13:24."

"I was visited by a happy, bearded fellow who carried a large bag over his shoulder this past Christmas," one woman said to her friend. "My son in college came home and brought his laundry."

Bruce sat on one end of the sofa, his girl friend on the other. For a long time neither spoke. Finally she said, "Bruce, do you think my eyes are beautiful?"

"Uh huh."

"And do you think my hair is the prettiest you ever saw?"

"Uh huh."

"Do you think I have a perfect figure?"

"You bet."

"Do you think my lips are like rubies?"

"Sure."

"Are my teeth like pearls?"

"I'll say."

"Oh, Bruce, you say the nicest things!"

A teenage girl was listening to her favorite punk rock group. As the song finished she said to her father, "Have you ever heard anything so great?"

The father replied, "Only one time, when a truck carrying empty milk cans hit another truck filled with live ducks."

A speaker for a large youth gathering said, "There are three things that are considered almost impossible:

1. Climbing a fence leaning toward you.
2. Kissing a girl who is leaning away from you.
3. Keeping the attention of a group of young people like this.

"Now, I've climbed a fence leaning toward me. I've kissed a girl leaning away from me. Now, let's prove the third impossibility is a possibility."

Homework—something teenagers do between phone calls.

It was one of those teenage weddings. When they got to the part of the ceremony where the boy repeats after the minister, "With all my worldly goods, I thee endow," the mother turned to the father and whispered, "There goes his bicycle."

A teenage boy came home from school one day with a note from one of his teachers saying she had to punish him for swearing. His father took him aside and asked, "Well, Son, what do you have to say?"

The boy answered, "I have nothing to say. I deserved it. She heard me say what she says she did and called me out into the hall."

"Well, what happened then?" asked his father.

"Well, she asked me where I had heard such terrible language. But I didn't want to give you away, Dad, so I blamed it on the parrot."

Two young men were looking for a book in a book store. One said to the other, "This looks awfully sad, *The Last Days of Pompeii*."

Said the other, "What did he die of?"

Ventured the first, "I'm really not sure but some form of eruption, I think."

A teenage magazine salesman was bragging to a friend about his success as a salesman.

"The reason that I'm a top producer is because I am sensitive to my customer's moods. I have empathy with my customers to the extent that I pretty well know what is on their minds at all times. For example, right now, I know what you are thinking."

"Really? Then why don't you get out of here?" his friend responded.

Back Then	Now
"Whatever may happen to thee, it was prepared for thee from all eternity; and the implication of causes was from eternity spinning the thread of thy being, and of that which is incident to it." (Marcus Aurelius Antonius)	"That's a bum deal."
"God's in his heaven— All's right with the world." (Robert Browning)	"For sure."
"Great is life . . . and real and mystical . . . wherever and whoever." (Walt Whitman)	"That's cool."
"I love thee to the depth and breadth and height/ My soul can reach" (Elizabeth Barrett Browning).	"You're too good for words."
"Joy was swept over my eyes . . . a fiery broom sweeping out of the skies like a star." (K. Wierzynski)	"Awesome!"
"Enough of love! If once I loved you, now is my youthful madness done." (Concepcion Valdes).	"I couldn't care less."

He: "I am a man of few words. Will you let me kiss you or won't you?"

She: "Usually, I would not. But you have talked me into it."

Time

Barbara: "Is your husband good at fixing things around the house?"

Jenny: "Well, I hate to complain, but since he fixed the clock, the cuckoo backs out and asks, 'What time is it?'"

A sugar planter in Hawaii took a tourist friend to the edge of a volcano. "That crater is 70,004 years old," he explained to the friend.

"How do you get the exact age?" asked the newcomer. "I can understand the seventy thousand, but where do you get the four?"

"Well," said the planter, "the volcano was 70,000 years old when I arrived, and I've been here four years."

The "good old days" were once known as "these trying times."

Going to work every morning just somehow breaks up the whole day.

For many years a minister had the reputation for his fine sermons which were not only inspirational, but unusually short.

When asked about his unusual awareness of time, he told this story:

"One Sunday I was delivering a sermon to my first congregation and I became so carried away by the sound of my own words that I didn't realize how restless people were becoming until a small boy, who had been squirming and fidgeting in the front pew, caught my attention. I saw him tug at his mother's sleeve and then, in a voice that could be heard throughout the church, he said, 'Mommy, are you sure this is the only way to get to heaven?'"

The man in the psychiatrist's office said, "I'd like to find out what makes me tick, doctor—and also what makes me chime the hour and the quarter hour, too!"

She: "It's only six o'clock. I told you to come after dinner."
He: "That's what I came after."

No wonder Rip Van Winkle was able to sleep twenty years; his neighbors didn't have stereo.

Boss: "Why do you never get to work on time anymore?"
Employee: "Well, you see, it's like this. You've warned me so long not to watch the clock here at the office that I've lost the habit of watching it at home."

Personnel manager: "How long did you work at your last place of employment?"
Applicant: "Forty-five years."
Personnel manager: "How old are you?"
Applicant: "Thirty-five years."
Personnel manager: "How could you work for forty-five years when you are only thirty-five years old?"
Applicant: "Overtime."

Convict: "How long are you in for?"
Cell Mate: "Ninety-nine years. How about you?"

Convict: "Seventy-five years."

Cell Mate: "Well, then, you take the bunk nearest the door; you're getting out first."

"Honey, a man came by today collecting clothes for the old clothes drive," explained a woman to her husband.

Inquired the husband, "Did you give him anything?"

"Yes, dear. I gave him that suit you've had for ten or twelve years and that dress I bought a few months ago."

"And here," announced the exhausted realtor as he showed the lady prospect through the eleventh house he had shown her. "This is the hobby room. Do you folks have any hobbies?"

"Oh, yes," replied the woman, "looking through model homes on Sundays!"

A woman went into an appliance store and told the salesman to show her some blenders. The salesman tried to sell her an expensive freezer instead.

"Really, Ma'am, this freezer will pay for itself in no time at all. Believe me, you can't go wrong with it."

"Good," said the lady. "As soon as it pays for itself you can deliver it."

The man and his wife arrived at the boarding gate in time to see their plane taking off. He was extremely upset about having missed the plane.

"If you weren't so slow in getting yourself ready we wouldn't have missed the plane," he complained.

"And if you hadn't rushed me so, we wouldn't have so long to wait for the next flight," she retorted.

A stitch in time saves embarrassment.

Travel

A most unnerving thing occurred at the airport yesterday. The pilot of the flight I was taking was in line ahead of me at the flight insurance counter.

A very thin, frail, old lady sat in a seat of a very crowded plane. She seemed to be very annoyed by the pressure upon her of an immensely fat lady who sat in the seat beside her.

Turning to her fat neighbor, the thin lady commented sweetly, "They really should charge by weight on airplanes."

Just as sweetly, the fat lady answered, "But if they did, they couldn't afford to stop for some people."

Lady to stewardess: "Tell the pilot not to fly faster than sound. My friend and I want to talk."

After buying a $100,000 insurance policy before a plane trip, a traveler received the following message in a fortune cookie, "A recent investment may pay big dividends."

On Lynn's first day back from her vacation a fellow employee asked, "How was your trip?"

"Well," she sighed, "have you ever spent three weeks in a van with those you thought you loved best?"

His wife kept nagging him to take her on a trip to the Thousand Islands. Finally, he compromised by taking her to Coney Island one thousand times.

He is a strong advocate of seat belts. He buckles himself in every time he drives his car, no matter how short the distance.

Recently, while his car was being serviced, he was driving a borrowed car which did not have seat belts.

Forgetting this, he parked in front of the bank, unbuckled his belt, stepped out of the car—and made a desperate grab for his pants.

A motorist was picked up unconscious after an accident and was being carried to a nearby service station. Opening his eyes, he began to kick and struggle desperately to get away. Afterwards, he explained that the first thing he saw was a "Shell" sign and somebody was standing in front of the "S"!

They have only two types of pedestrians in most cities—the quick and the dead.

A fellow bought a Rolls Royce. The first day he had it, his wife said, "Be an angel and let me drive."

So he did, and he is.

A panhandler approached a state department official in Washington, D.C. "Please," he begged, "give me $300 for a cup of coffee."

"But coffee is only a dime," said the official.

"I know," said the panhandler, "but I want to drink mine in Brazil."

Man (showing a snapshot of himself with a fish to his neighbor): "My daughter caught the biggest fish on our vacation—a young man twenty-four years old!"

Hotel guest (over telephone): "Is this the manager?"
Annoyed manager: "Yes, it is. What's eating you?"
Guest: "That's what I would like to know!"

A guest in a small, country inn was paying for his room. "Did you know that the room you stayed in was once used by Wellington?" asked the desk clerk.

"You don't say!" said the guest. "Did he use the same bed?"

"I believe he did!" said the clerk, wanting to please.

"Well, now I know why he was called the 'Iron Duke!'"

"Don't be so down in the dumps," said a sailor to a passenger. "Seasickness never killed anyone."

Moaned the sick passenger, "Please don't say that. It's only the hope of dying that has kept me alive so far!"

Timid airplane passenger: "Stewardess, how often do big jets like this one crash?"

Stewardess: "As a rule—only once."

There was a motel guest who found his bed already occupied by an all but invisible intruder, and he wrote a protest against insect-infected beds. By return mail he received such a gracious apology that he was ashamed of having made a fuss about such a trifling matter and said so in another letter. Turning over the company's letter to get the writer's name, he came upon this penciled notation: "Send this guy the bug letter E-w3, 8w5."

A passenger in a commuter plane was amazed when the pilot began to laugh uncontrollably. "What's so funny?" asked the passenger.

"I'm thinking of what they will say at the asylum when they find out I have escaped," said the pilot.

My new car has bucket seats. They are really comfortable as long as your bucket isn't too large.

A man called the station master, "I left a bottle of white lightning on the train. I was wondering if it turned up in the lost and found department?"

"No, Sir, but the fellow who found it did."

Wealth

Formula to get rich: "Buy fifty female pigs and fifty male deer and put them together and have you one hundred sows and bucks."

A very wealthy man suddenly clutched his chest and yelled to his wife, "I think I'm having a heart attack! Don't just stand there, buy me a hospital!"

A stranger strolled into a doctor's office and said, "Doc, I just stopped by to tell you how much I benefited from your treatments."

"But you aren't a patient of mine," replied the bewildered doctor.

"Yes, I know, but my great uncle was, and I'm his heir."

The legislators in several towns are pondering a law limiting local merchants to only one "going out of business" sale a year.

A class of students was watching the professor of chemistry give a demonstration of the properties of various acids.

"Now I am going to drop this half dollar into this glass of acid," said the professor. "Will it dissolve?"

"No, Sir," replied one of the students.

"No? Then would you like to explain to the rest of the class why it won't dissolve."

The student replied, "Because, if the half dollar would dissolve you wouldn't drop it in."

"Now Maggie," the lady said, "remember that when the queen arrives you must say, 'Your grace.'"

The moment arrived. Maggie hurried to the door, opened it and solemnly said, "May the Lord make us truly grateful for what we are about to receive."

Teacher: "Where is the capital of the United States?"
Student: "All over Europe!"

Son: "How much am I worth?"
Father: "Son, you are worth a million dollars to me."
Son: "Well, do you think you could advance me about ten dollars?"

First man: "My wife dreamed last night she was married to a millionaire!"
Second man: "You're lucky. My wife thinks that in the daytime!"

"I have nothing but praise for our new pastor."
"Yeah—I noticed that when they passed the offering plate."

> To get his wealth, he spent his health,
> and then, with strength and main,
> He turned around and spent his wealth
> to get his health again.

He's always dating his checks ahead. If he should die, say on April 30, his tombstone will probably read, "HE DIED APRIL 30, AS OF MAY 15."

Advised to get a job, invest his earnings, and accumulate capital so that one day he wouldn't have to work anymore, he replied, "Why should I go through all that? I'm not working now."

She asked her husband for ten dollars. "What did you do with the ten dollars I gave you yesterday—serial number C958439-G?" he demanded.

It's amazing how he always manages to be away from the table when the waitress brings the check—no wonder his nickname is "After-Dinner Sneaker."

His car is so old, his insurance policy covers theft, fire, and Indian raids.

He recently bought some shirts cheap and changed his name to go with the monogram.

Three people gathered at the casket of a friend. The first said, "In my country it is believed that if one places a little money in the casket, it will ease the departed one's journey." Then he placed ten dollars in the coffin. The second did the same thing. The third man wrote a check for thirty dollars and took the two tens.

Judge: "I notice that in addition to stealing money, you also took rings, watches, diamonds, and pearls."
Prisoner: "Yes, sir. I was always taught that money alone doesn't bring happiness."

Wit and Wisdom

The prime cause of problems is solutions.

Those who are unable to learn from past meetings are doomed to repeat them.

Eleventh Commandment: Thou shalt not committee.

A committee is ten people doing the work of one.

Two monologues don't make a dialogue.

Everyone who doesn't work has a plan that does.

No two identical parts are the same.

Nothing is as permanent as that which they call temporary.

History repeats itself. That is what is wrong with history.

He who hesitates is more than likely right.

If all else fails, try the boss's idea.

You can't fall off the floor.

Any horizontal surface is soon piled up.

A clean tie always attracts the soup of the day.

The hardness of the butter is inversely proportional to the softness of the bread.

When a person is immersed in water, the telephone always rings.

The grocery bag that breaks is always the one with the eggs in it.

When packing for a trip, take half as much clothing and twice as much money.

Chipped dishes never break.

When there are adequate funds in the checking account, checks take a week to clear. When there are inadequate funds in the checking account, they clear overnight.

The book you paid $12.95 for today will probably come out in paperback tomorrow.

The more an item costs, the further you have to send it to have it repaired.

When it says, "one size fits all," it never fits anybody.

The quicker you fall behind, the more time you have to catch up.

In an otherwise empty locker room, some two people will have connecting lockers.

The colder the X-ray table, the more of your body you have to put on it.

You remember to mail the letter only when you're not close to a mailbox.

When you drop change at a vending machine, the pennies fall nearby, while all other coins roll out of sight.

Wind velocity increases directly with the cost of the hairdo.

For every "10" there are usually ten "1's."

Everybody is someone else's weirdo.

Everyone wants to peel his own banana.

People are divided into two groups—the righteous and the unrighteous—and the righteous usually do the dividing.

The severity of the itch is inversely proportional to the reach.

Those who live the closest always arrive latest.

Experience is something you usually don't get until after you need it.

Most well-trodden paths lead nowhere.

The only people who find what they are looking for in life are the faultfinders.

You can observe a lot just by watching.

Whatever goes around, comes around.

You can't push on a rope.

There is no such thing as instant experience.

Women

The only time Doris ever told her true age was on an African safari when she was captured by a picky cannibal who never ate anyone over forty.

I know a woman who talks so much she was married for two years before she found out her husband was deaf and dumb.

"I hate to think my wife gets her own way," confessed one man to his friend, "but she always writes in her diary a week ahead of time!"

Ralph: "Is your wife broad-minded?"
Frank: "She sure is. She believes there are two sides to every argument—hers and her mother's."

A braggart was telling everyone that he could bend a horseshoe with his bare hands. After listening for awhile one man stood up and said, "That's nothing. My wife can tie up five miles of telephone wire with her chin!"

Gary: "My wife and I have a joint checking account."
Jeff: "Isn't that confusing?"
Gary: "No. I put the money in, and she takes it out."

The wife of a young engineer who was away on a trip to Alaska knitted him a warm sweater which she mailed with the following letter: "Postage costs so much that I cut off the buttons. Love and kisses. P. S. The buttons are in the left-hand pocket."

Seven ages of women: Baby, infant, young miss, young woman, young woman, young woman, young woman.

Sam: "Have you ever suspected your wife of living a double life?"
Herb: "Yes, her own and mine."

Some women leave their husbands and take everything. Others take everything, but never leave.

Leon: "Does your wife pick your clothes?"
Ron: "No, only the pockets."

Mrs. Bowen (handing her husband a dish of white powder): "Dear, taste this and tell me what you think it is."

Mr. Bowen (tasting it): "It tastes like soda."

Mrs. Bowen: "That's what I told Margaret. But she declares it is rat poison. Taste it again to make sure."

You really can't raise an eyebrow when she says she's only thirty. Anybody who stays with the same story for ten years has to be telling the truth.

When her husband isn't home she goes over to the neighbors and insults them—just to keep in practice.

She's just about truthful. She doesn't lie about anything except her weight, her age, and her husband's annual earnings.

She speaks 150 words per minute—with gusts up to 190.

He always has a voice in what she purchases—the invoice.

Byron: "My wife and I always think exactly the same. Only she always has the first think."

Thinking it would be fun to surprise her husband at the office, a woman bought a new wig. She walked in his office and said, "Do you think there is room in your life for a woman like me?"

"No way," he reported, "you remind me too much of my wife."

The only problem with being a woman these days is you have to look like a young girl, dress like a boy, think like a man, and work like a dog.

Horse sense is what keeps a woman from becoming a nag.

Wonder how many fig leaves Eve tried on before she said, "I'll take this one."

As the three ladies picked up a menu, each put on a pair of glasses.

"I really only need mine for close reading," explained the first.

Remarked the second, "I only wear mine when the lighting is bad."

The third confessed, "I rarely wear mine—except when I want to see."

Wife (to husband on Christmas morning): "You angel! This is just what I need to exchange for just what I wanted!"

A movie producer was telling a friend about giving his girlfriend a string of pearls for her birthday. "Why," said his friend, "don't you give her something practical—like a car?"

The producer smiled and said, "Did you ever hear of a phony automobile?"

Mr. Henpeck: "Haven't I always given you my paycheck the first of every month?"

Mrs. Henpeck: "Yes, but you also never told me you got paid on the first *and* the fifteenth!"

When it comes to keeping house, she likes to do nothing better.

Where there is smoke there she is—cooking.

It always astonishes him that she can see right through him—yet she can't see a button missing off his coat.

She serves blended coffee—yesterday's and today's.

One night his wife whispered, "There's a burglar in the kitchen. He's eating the casserole I made for dinner."
He replied. "Go back to sleep. I'll bury him first thing in the morning."

She has one solid theory in the kitchen—if it does not move, wrap it in plastic wrap.

He married her because he wanted someone to cook and clean house for him. The problem is, she married him for the same reasons.

Tammy: "What did you do in England?"
Pam: "I went boating on the Thames."
Tammy: "Well, I've been there. Passed through on my way to Stratford-on-Avon. It was good to see where those door-to-door products come from."

Miscellaneous

One casket to another: "Is that you coffin?"

Salesman to housewife: "This freezer will pay for itself with what you save on your food bills."

Housewife: "That may be, but with the money we are saving on taxi fare we are buying a car, paying for a washer with the laundry bills we save, and from the money we are saving on rent we are paying for the house. We just can't afford to save any more right now."

Barber: "Haven't I shaved you before, Sir?"
Customer: "No, I got that scar in Vietnam."

What do fish and guests have in common? They both smell after three days.

Critic: "That's a very graceful statue, but isn't that an odd position for a general to assume?"
Sculptor: "Perhaps it is. But, you see, I was half finished when the committee decided they couldn't afford a horse for him."

A large family visited the zoo. Upon arriving they found the admission was one dollar per family. The father guided his twelve children through the gate and handed the ticket collector a dollar bill.

"Are all these your children?" he asked.

"Sure are," replied the proud father.

"Then take your dollar back. It's worth more for the animals to see your family than for your family to see the animals."

"Do you know Buck James?"

"Of course I do—we've slept in the same pew at church together for the last fifteen years!"

He's so polite he even says "Thank you" when an automatic door opens for him.

A mischievous young boy tied the tails of two cats together and threw them into the basement of the church. The cats clawed and yowled all during the week, but the neighbors did not pay any attention, they just thought it was the choir practicing.

When fire broke out in a building across the street from a hospital where a man was undergoing surgery, the doctor, knowing what kind of life his patient had led, said to the attending nurse, "Pull down that window shade, or when he comes to he will think the operation was unsuccessful."

Old Mr. Johnson never told a lie, but he did tell this story: He was standing by a pond one day and saw a large garter snake attack an enormous bullfrog. The snake seized the frog's hind legs and the frog caught the snake by the tail. Both commenced swallowing each other and continued this carnivorous operation until nothing was left of them.

Teacher: "Who was the smartest inventor?"
Student: "Thomas Edison."
Teacher: "Why is that?"
Student: "Because he invented the stereo and radio so people would stay up all night and use his electric light bulbs."

"Pastor, is it a sin to play golf on Sunday?"
"Son, I've seen you play, and it's a sin for you to play any day of the week."

A fellow was playing golf with his priest, and he noticed that before every shot the priest would say a prayer.
"Father, would it help me to pray?"
"No. I'm afraid not."
"But why?"
"Because you are a terrible putter."

Wife: "Henry, you promised you'd be home at 4:00. Now it's 8:00."

Husband: "Honey, please listen to me. Poor ole' Fred is dead, just dropped over on the eighth green."

Wife: "Oh, that's awful."

Husband: "It surely was. For the rest of the game it was hit the ball, drag Fred, hit the ball, drag Fred."

"What's your golf handicap?"

"I'm too honest."

I hate taking naps. Waking up once a day is bad enough.

Television was better in the old days before it had pictures and sound.

Did you know that "sdrawkcab" is "backwards" spelled backwards?

Mugger: "This is a holdup! Give me your money or else."

Victim: "Or else what?"

Mugger: "Don't confuse me. This is my first holdup."

Young Dobbs had just moved into his new office and was waiting for his first client. Suddenly, footsteps were heard coming down the hall, heading for his office. Quickly, the new bar member sat down behind his desk, picked up the phone, and began talking to nobody.

"Well," said Dobbs, "I'm really quite busy right now, and I've got to be in court this afternoon and again tomorrow. Then I have an appointment with clients tomorrow afternoon and the next day, too."

He looked up to see a man standing at the door watching, then he continued his make-believe conversation to make sure he impressed the man.

He said into the phone, "Maybe I can squeeze you in on Friday afternoon. All right. See you then."

Dobbs hung up the telephone and turned to the man at the door. "Yes, can I help you?"

"No," the man replied, "I just came to connect your telephone."